FEDERAL FIREFIGHTER FUNDING AND FIRE ASSISTANCE

GOVERNMENT PROCEDURES AND OPERATIONS

Additional books in this series can be found on Nova's website
under the Series tab.

Additional E-books in this series can be found on Nova's website
under the e-books tab.

SAFETY AND RISK IN SOCIETY

Additional books in this series can be found on Nova's website
under the Series tab.

Additional E-books in this series can be found on Nova's website
under the e-books tab.

GOVERNMENT PROCEDURES AND OPERATIONS

FEDERAL FIREFIGHTER FUNDING AND FIRE ASSISTANCE

MASON L. HILL

AND

CHRISTOPHER F. GREEN

EDITORS

Nova Science Publishers, Inc.

New York

NOTICE TO THE READER

Library of Congress Cataloging-in-Publication Data

ISBN: 978-1-62081-176-4

Published by Nova Science Publishers, Inc. † New York

CONTENTS

PREFACE

Firefighting activities are traditionally the responsibility of states and local communities. As such, funding for firefighters is provided mostly by state and local governments. During the 1990s, shortfalls in state and local budgets, coupled with increased responsibilities of local fire departments, led many in the fire community to call for additional financial support from the federal government. This book provides an overview on the distribution of fire grant funding; the SAFER Grant program; and federal funding for wildfire control and management.

Chapter 1 - The Assistance to Firefighters Grant (AFG) Program, also known as fire grants or the FIRE Act grant program, was established by Title XVII of the FY2001 National Defense Authorization Act (P.L. 106-398). Currently administered by the Federal Emergency Management Agency (FEMA), Department of Homeland Security (DHS), the program provides federal grants directly to local fire departments and unaffiliated Emergency Medical Services (EMS) organizations to help address a variety of equipment, training, and other firefighter-related and EMS needs. A related program is the Staffing for Adequate Fire and Emergency Response Firefighters (SAFER) program, which provides grants for hiring, recruiting, and retaining firefighters.

The fire grant program is now in its 12th year. The Fire Act statute was reauthorized in 2004 (Title XXXVI of P.L. 108-375) and provides overall guidelines on how fire grant money should be distributed. There is no set geographical formula for the distribution of fire grants—fire departments throughout the nation apply, and award decisions are made by a peer panel based on the merits of the application and the needs of the community. However, the law does require that fire grants be distributed to a diverse mix of fire departments, with respect to type of department (paid, volunteer, or combination), geographic location, and type of community served (e.g., urban, suburban, or rural).

The full-year continuing appropriation bill for FY2011, which was signed into law on April 15, 2011 (Department of Defense and Continuing Appropriations Act, 2011, P.L. 112-10) funded AFG at $405 million and SAFER at $405 million for FY2011.

The administration's FY2012 budget proposed $670 million for firefighter assistance, including $250 million for AFG and $420 million for SAFER. According to the budget proposal, the request would fund 2,200 firefighter positions and approximately 5,000 AFG grants. P.L. 112-74, the Consolidated Appropriations Act, FY2012 provides $675 million for firefighter assistance, including $337.5 million for AFG and $337.5 million for SAFER.

On March 10, 2011, S. 550, the Fire Grants Authorization Act of 2011 was introduced into the 112th Congress. Previously in the 111th Congress, reauthorization legislation for AFG and SAFER was passed by the House, but was not passed by the Senate. Debate over the reauthorization reflected a competition for funding between career/urban/suburban departments and volunteer/rural departments. The urgency of this debate was heightened by the proposed reduction of overall AFG funding in FY2011, and the economic downturn in many local communities increasingly hard pressed to allocate funding for their local fire departments.

On June 22, 2011, H.R. 2269, the Fire Grants Reauthorization Act of 2011, was introduced into the 112th Congress. H.R. 2269 is virtually identical to House legislation that was passed in the 111th Congress.

Chapter 2 - In response to concerns over the adequacy of firefighter staffing, the Staffing for Adequate Fire and Emergency Response Act—popularly called the "SAFER Act"—was enacted by the 108th Congress as Section 1057 of the FY2004 National Defense Authorization Act (P.L. 108-136). The SAFER Act authorizes grants to career, volunteer, and combination local fire departments for the purpose of increasing the number of firefighters to help communities meet industry-minimum standards and attain 24-hour staffing to provide adequate protection from fire and fire-related hazards. Also authorized are grants to volunteer fire departments for recruitment and retention of volunteers.

With the economic turndown adversely affecting budgets of local governments, concerns have arisen that modifications to the SAFER statute may be necessary to enable fire departments to more effectively participate in the program. The American Recovery and Reinvestment Act of 2009 (P.L.

111-5) included a provision (§603) that waived the matching requirements for SAFER grants awarded in FY2009 and FY2010. The FY2009 Supplemental Appropriations Act (P.L. 111- 32) included a provision authorizing the Secretary of Homeland Security to waive further limitations and restrictions in the SAFER statute for FY2009 and FY2010.

The Department of Defense and Continuing Appropriations Act, 2011 (P.L. 112-10) funded SAFER at $405 million. The law also contained language that removes cost-share requirements and allows SAFER grants to be used to rehire laid-off firefighters and fill positions eliminated through attrition. However, P.L. 112-10 did not remove the requirement that SAFER grants fund a firefighter position for four years, with the fifth year funded wholly by the grant recipient. The law also did not waive the cap of $100,000 per firefighter hired by a SAFER grant.

The Administration's FY2012 budget proposed $670 million for firefighter assistance, including $420 million for SAFER, which according to the FY2012 budget proposal, would fund 2,200 firefighter positions. P.L. 112-74, the Consolidated Appropriations Act, FY2012 provided $337.5 million for SAFER, and included language permitting FY2012 grants to be used to rehire laid-off firefighters and fill positions eliminated through attrition, as well as removing other SAFER restrictions and limitations. P.L. 112-74 also reinstated waiver authority for the restrictions that were not lifted in the FY2011 appropriations act (P.L. 112-10).

Concern over local fire departments' budgetary problems has framed debate over the SAFER reauthorization, which is included in S. 550/H.R. 2269, the Fire Grants Authorization Act of 2011. Previously in the 111th Congress, reauthorization legislation for SAFER was passed by the House, but was not passed by the Senate. As part of the reauthorization debate, Congress may consider whether some SAFER rules and restrictions governing the hiring grants should be eliminated or altered in order to make it economically feasible for more fire departments to participate in the program.

Chapter 3 - The Forest Service (FS) and the Department of the Interior (DOI) are responsible for protecting most federal lands from wildfires. Wildfire appropriations nearly doubled in FY2001, following a severe fire season in the summer of 2000, and have remained at relatively high levels. The acres burned annually have also increased over the past 50 years, with the six highest annual totals occurring since 2000. Many in Congress are concerned that wildfire costs are spiraling upward without a reduction in damages. With emergency supplemental funding, FY2008 wildfire funding was $4.46 billion, more than in any previous year.

The vast majority (about 95%) of federal wildfire funds are spent to protect federal lands—for fire preparedness (equipment, baseline personnel, and training); fire suppression operations (including emergency funding); post-fire rehabilitation (to help sites recover after the wildfire); and fuel reduction (to reduce wildfire damages by reducing fuel levels). Since FY2001, FS fire appropriations have included funds for state fire assistance, volunteer fire assistance, and forest health management (to supplement other funds for these three programs), economic action and community assistance, fire research, and fire facilities.

Four issues have dominated wildfire funding debates. One is the high cost of fire management and its effects on other agency programs. Several studies have recommended actions to try to control wildfire costs, and the agencies have taken various steps, but it is unclear whether these actions will be sufficient. Borrowing to pay high wildfire suppression costs has affected other agency programs. The Federal Land Assistance, Management, and Enhancement (FLAME) Act was enacted in P.L. 111-88 to insulate other agency programs from high wildfire suppression costs by creating a separate funding structure for emergency supplemental wildfire suppression efforts.

Another issue is funding for fuel reduction. Funding and acres treated rose (roughly doubling) between FY2000 and FY2003, and have stabilized since. Currently about 3 million acres are treated annually. However, 75 million acres of federal land are at high risk, and another 156 million acres are at moderate risk, of ecological damage from catastrophic wildfire. Since many ecosystems need to be treated on a 10-35 year cycle (depending on the ecosystem), current treatment rates are insufficient to address the problem.

A third issue is the federal role in protecting nonfederal lands, communities, and private structures. In 1994, federal firefighting resources were apparently used to protect private residences at a cost to federal lands and resources in one severe fire. A federal policy review recommended increased state and local efforts to match their responsibilities, but federal programs to protect nonfederal lands have also expanded, reducing incentives for local participation in fire protection.

Finally, post-fire rehabilitation is raising concerns. Agency regulations and legislation in the 109th Congress focused on expediting such activities, but opponents expressed concerns that this would restrict environmental review of and public involvement in salvage logging decisions, leading to greater environmental damage. Legislation was introduced but not enacted in the 110th Congress to provide alternative means of addressing post-fire restoration in particular areas. The large wildfires to date in 2011 have reignited concerns about post-fire rehabilitation.

Chapter 4 - Raging wildfires, burned homes, and the evacuation of thousands make headlines nearly every fire season. Severe wildfires in 2011 occurred in Arizona and New Mexico in the late spring, and in Texas and Arizona in the late summer. Options for federal support and assistance— during the fires, in the aftermath, and aimed at preventing a recurrence—have been raised by many concerned about the ongoing disasters. This report briefly describes these federal options.

Chapter 5 - The U.S. Fire Administration (USFA)—which includes the National Fire Academy (NFA)—is currently housed within the Federal Emergency Management Agency (FEMA) of the Department of Homeland Security (DHS). The objective of the USFA is to significantly reduce the nation's loss of life from fire, while also achieving a reduction in property loss and non-fatal injury due to fire. The United States Fire Administration Reauthorization Act of 2008 was signed into law on October 8, 2008 (P.L. 110-376).

The Department of Defense and Continuing Appropriations Act, 2011 (P.L. 112-10) funded USFA at $45.588 million, the same as the FY2010 level. The FY2012 budget proposal requested $42.538 million for USFA, about 7% under the FY2011 level. The budget proposal reflected an overall $1.72 million program reduction. P.L. 112-74, the Consolidated Appropriations Act, FY2012, provided $44.038 million for USFA in FY2012.

As is the case with many federal programs, concerns in the 112th Congress over the federal budget deficit could impact budget levels for the USFA. Debate over the USFA budget has focused on whether the USFA is receiving an appropriate level of funding to accomplish its mission, given that appropriations for USFA have consistently been well below the agency's authorized level. An ongoing issue is the viability and status of the USFA and National Fire Academy within the Department of Homeland Security.

In: Federal Firefighter Funding and Fire Assistance   ISBN 978-1-62081-176-4
Editors: M. L. Hill and C. F. Green   ©2012 Nova Science Publishers, Inc.

Chapter 1

ASSISTANCE TO FIREFIGHTERS PROGRAM: DISTRIBUTION OF FIRE GRANT FUNDING[*]

Lennard G. Kruger

SUMMARY

The Assistance to Firefighters Grant (AFG) Program, also known as
fire grants or the FIRE Act grant program, was established by Title XVII
of the FY2001 National Defense Authorization Act (P.L. 106-398).
Currently administered by the Federal Emergency Management Agency
(FEMA), Department of Homeland Security (DHS), the program
provides federal grants directly to local fire departments and unaffiliated
Emergency Medical Services (EMS) organizations to help address a
variety of equipment, training, and other firefighter-related and EMS
needs. A related program is the Staffing for Adequate Fire and
Emergency Response Firefighters (SAFER) program, which provides
grants for hiring, recruiting, and retaining firefighters.

The fire grant program is now in its 12th year. The Fire Act statute
was reauthorized in 2004 (Title XXXVI of P.L. 108-375) and provides
overall guidelines on how fire grant money should be distributed. There is
no set geographical formula for the distribution of fire grants—fire
departments throughout the nation apply, and award decisions are made
by a peer panel based on the merits of the application and the needs of the
community. However, the law does require that fire grants be distributed

---

[*] This is an edited, reformatted and augmented version of Congressional Research Service, Publication No. RL32341, dated January 3, 2012.

to a diverse mix of fire departments, with respect to type of department (paid, volunteer, or combination), geographic location, and type of community served (e.g., urban, suburban, or rural).

The full-year continuing appropriation bill for FY2011, which was signed into law on April 15, 2011 (Department of Defense and Continuing Appropriations Act, 2011, P.L. 112-10) funded AFG at $405 million and SAFER at $405 million for FY2011.

The administration's FY2012 budget proposed $670 million for firefighter assistance, including $250 million for AFG and $420 million for SAFER. According to the budget proposal, the request would fund 2,200 firefighter positions and approximately 5,000 AFG grants. P.L. 112-74, the Consolidated Appropriations Act, FY2012 provides $675 million for firefighter assistance, including $337.5 million for AFG and $337.5 million for SAFER.

On March 10, 2011, S. 550, the Fire Grants Authorization Act of 2011 was introduced into the 112th Congress. Previously in the 111th Congress, reauthorization legislation for AFG and SAFER was passed by the House, but was not passed by the Senate. Debate over the reauthorization reflected a competition for funding between career/urban/suburban departments and volunteer/rural departments. The urgency of this debate was heightened by the proposed reduction of overall AFG funding in FY2011, and the economic downturn in many local communities increasingly hard pressed to allocate funding for their local fire departments.

On June 22, 2011, H.R. 2269, the Fire Grants Reauthorization Act of 2011, was introduced into the 112th Congress. H.R. 2269 is virtually identical to House legislation that was passed in the 111th Congress.

BACKGROUND

Firefighting activities are traditionally the responsibility of states and local communities. As such, funding for firefighters is provided mostly by state and local governments. During the 1990s, shortfalls in state and local budgets, coupled with increased responsibilities of local fire departments, led many in the fire community to call for additional financial support from the federal government. Although federally funded training programs existed (and continue to exist) through the National Fire Academy, and although federal money was available to first responders for counterterrorism training and equipment through the Department of Justice,[1] there did not exist a dedicated program, exclusively for firefighters, which provided federal money directly to local fire departments to help address a wide variety of equipment, training, and other firefighter-related needs.

ASSISTANCE TO FIREFIGHTERS GRANT PROGRAM

During the 106th Congress, many in the fire community asserted that local fire departments require and deserve greater support from the federal government. The Assistance to Firefighters Grant Program (AFG), also known as fire grants or the FIRE Act grant program, was established by Title XVII of the FY2001 Floyd D. Spence National Defense Authorization Act (P.L. 106-398).[2] Currently administered by the Federal Emergency Management Agency (FEMA) in the Department of Homeland Security (DHS), the program provides federal grants directly to local fire departments and unaffiliated Emergency Medical Services (EMS) organizations to help address a variety of equipment, training, and other firefighter-related and EMS needs.

Reauthorization Act of 2004

On October 28, 2004, the President signed the FY2005 Ronald W. Reagan National Defense Authorization Act (P.L. 108-375). Title XXXVI of P.L. 108-375 is the Assistance to Firefighters Grant Program Reauthorization Act of 2004, which reauthorized the fire grant program through FY2009. Table 1 provides a summary of key provisions of the 2004 reauthorization.

Current Reauthorization

The most recent authorization of AFG expired on September 30, 2009; the authorization of SAFER expired September 30, 2010. Previously in the 111th Congress, reauthorization legislation for AFG and SAFER was passed by the House, but was not passed by the Senate. In the 112th Congress, the Senate reauthorization bill for AFG and SAFER been reintroduced as S. 550. The House bill has been reintroduced as H.R. 2269.

Table 1. Major Provisions of the Assistance to Firefighters Grant Program Reauthorization Act of 2004

Grant recipient limits: populations over 1 million—lesser of $2.75 million or 0.5% of total appropriation populations of 500K to 1 million—$1.75 million populations under 500K—$1 million no single grant can exceed 0.5% of total funds appropriated for a single fiscal year DHS can waive the funding limits for populations up to 1 million in instances of extraordinary need; however the lesser of $2.75 million or 0.5% limit cannot be waived
Nonfederal match requirements: 20% for populations over 50K 10% for populations 20K to 50K 5% for populations less than 20K No match requirement for non-fire department prevention and firefighter safety grants
Authorized for five years: FY2005—$900 million FY2006—$950 million FY2007—$1 billion FY2008—$1 billion FY2009—$1 billion
Expands grant eligibility to emergency medical service squads, not less than 3.5% of fire grant money for EMS, but no more than 2% for nonaffiliated EMS
Provides grants for firefighter health and safety R&D
Requires the USFA Administrator to convene an annual meeting of non-federal fire service experts to recommend criteria for awarding grants and administrative changes
Requires fire service peer review of grant applications
Requires the USFA, in conjunction with the National Fire Protection Association, to conduct a $300,000, 18-month study on the fire grant program and the need for federal assistance to state and local communities to fund firefighting and emergency response activities

Source: Assistance to Firefighters Grant Program Reauthorization Act of 2004, Section XXXVI of P.L. 108-375, FY2005 Ronald W. Reagan National Defense Authorization Act.

House Reauthorization Bill: 111ᵗʰ Congress

On July 8, 2009, the House Committee on Science and Technology, Subcommittee on Technology & Innovation, held a hearing on the reauthorization of the FIRE grant programs (both AFG and SAFER).[3] Testimony was heard from FEMA and many of the major fire service organizations including the International Association of Fire Chiefs (IAFC), the International Association of Fire Fighters (IAFF), the National Volunteer Fire Council (NVFC), and the National Fire Protection Association (NFPA).

A major issue surrounding the fire grant reauthorization is whether the current distribution of fire grant funds should be altered. Under current law, the majority of funding goes to rural and volunteer fire departments. This is the case because individual fire departments throughout the nation apply directly for funding, and there are many more volunteer and rural fire departments than career and urban/suburban fire departments.[4] In general, career departments tend to protect the more densely populated urban and suburban areas, while volunteer departments tend to protect more rural areas.

Testimony presented by the International Association of Fire Fighters (IAFF), representing career (paid) firefighters, argued that under current law, "the overwhelming majority of FIRE grants are awarded to fire departments that protect a relatively small percentage of the population."[5] According to IAFF, a greater proportion of funding should go to career fire departments protecting the more densely populated suburban and urban areas, and suggested the following changes in the fire act statute:

- professional, volunteer, and combination departments should each be guaranteed at least 30% of total grant funding each year (under current statute, volunteer and combination departments must receive *no less* than 55% of funding; in practice career departments have received about 20% of AFG funding);
- funding caps for a single grant should be raised to $10 million for communities of 1 million population or more, $5 million for communities of 500,000 or more, $2 million for communities of 100,000 or more, and $1 million for communities with populations under 100,000 (current statutory caps are $2.75 million for populations over 1 million, $1.75 million for populations over 500,000, and $1 million for populations under 500,000); and
- the local match requirement for fire grants should be set at 15% for all applicants, with DHS having the authority to waive the match requirement for needy departments (the current statutory matching requirements are 20% for populations over 50,000, 10% for populations over 20,000, and 5% for populations less than 20,000).[6]

On the other hand, testimony from the National Volunteer Fire Council (NFVC) stated that its main priority for reauthorization of AFG (as well as SAFER) is to extend the programs without substantial changes, and that "the programs are well-run, distributing funding in an efficient manner to the most deserving awardees."[7] NVFC argued that volunteer departments are concentrated in rural communities with smaller tax bases and higher poverty rates, that "DHS needs assessments have consistently shown that equipment training and apparatus needs are most acute in volunteer departments,"[8] and that since 2001 DHS first responder grants for terrorism and disaster response have predominantly gone to urban areas.

Meanwhile, other suggested reauthorization changes to the AFG statute made by the July 8 hearing witnesses included

- establish DHS waiver authority for the existing local match requirement for economically challenged jurisdictions (IAFC);
- establish centers of excellence in fire safety research (IAFC);
- allow larger grants for regional projects (IAFC);
- eliminate the cost-share requirement for fire departments in the Fire Prevention and Firefighter Safety grant program (NFPA and IAFF);
- designate a minimum of 5% of funding for fire service-based emergency medical services (NFPA);
- utilize funds for training and equipment to meet the latest applicable national voluntary consensus standards available at the time of application (NFPA); and
- make state training agencies (e.g., state fire academies) eligible for AFG funding (NVFC).

As manifested in the July 8 hearing, debate over the AFG reauthorization reflected a competition for funding primarily between career/urban/suburban departments and volunteer/rural departments. The urgency of this debate was heightened by reductions in FY2010 AFG funding and by the economic downturn in many local communities increasingly hard pressed to allocate funding for their local fire departments.

On October 13, 2009, H.R. 3791, the Fire Grants Reauthorization Act of 2009, was introduced by Representative Mitchell. The legislation reflected an agreement reached among the major fire service organizations on the reauthorization language. H.R. 3791 was referred to the House Committee on Science and Technology, and approved (amended) by the Subcommittee on Technology and Innovation on October 14, 2009, and by the full committee on October 21, 2009. H.R. 3791 was reported (amended) by the committee on November 7, 2009 (H.Rept. 111-333, Part I). H.R. 3791 was amended and passed by the House on November 18, 2009. Adopted amendments included directing DHS to conduct a survey of fire department compliance with firefighter safety standards; requiring DHS to give added consideration to applications from areas with high unemployment; making river rescue organizations eligible for funding; expanding AFG scope to include equipment that reduces water use; and prohibiting earmarking of funds appropriated under the act.

H.R. 3791, as passed by the House, would have authorized AFG at a level of $1 billion per year through FY2014 and included the following major provisions:

- *Grant Money Distribution*—directs that grant money should be allocated (to the extent that there are eligible applicants) as follows: 25% of AFG funding to career fire departments; 25% to volunteer fire departments; 25% to combination fire departments; 10% (minimum) for fire prevention, safety, and research grants; 2% (maximum) for volunteer non-fire service EMS and rescue; 3% (maximum) for fire service training academies; and 10% to be competitive between career, volunteer and combination departments;
- *Grant Caps*—sets maximum individual grant levels at $9 million for jurisdictions with populations over 2.5 million, $6 million for populations between 1 million and 2.5 million, $3 million for populations between 500,000 and 1 million, $2 million for populations between 100,000 and 500,000, and $1 million for populations under 100,000;
- *Matching Requirements*—keeps the existing 5% matching requirement for communities of 20K or less, sets the matching requirement for all other jurisdictions at 10%, and allows an economic hardship waiver whereby in "exceptional circumstances" DHS may waive or reduce the matching requirements;
- *Maintenance of Expenditures*—amends the existing maintenance of expenditures provision to require applicants to maintain budgets at 80% of the average over the past two years, also allows an economic hardship waiver whereby in "exceptional circumstances" DHS may waive or reduce the maintenance of expenditures requirements;
- *Fire Prevention, Research, and Safety Grants*—increases available funding from 5% to 10% of total, raises grant maximum from $1 million to $1.5 million, eliminates the matching requirement for fire departments, and prohibits any funding to the Association of Community Organizations for Reform Now (ACORN);
- *University Fire Safety Research Centers*—as part of the fire prevention, research, and safety grants, authorizes DHS to establish

no more than three university fire safety research centers with funding of any one center at not more than $2 million per fiscal year;

- *State Fire Training Academies*—allows DHS to award up to 3% of grant funding to state fire training academies, with individual grants not to exceed $1 million;
- *Voluntary Consensus Standards*—directs that grants used for training should be limited to training that complies with applicable national voluntary consensus standards, unless a waiver has been granted; and
- *Survey and Task Force on Firefighter Safety*—directs DHS to conduct a nationwide survey to assess whether fire departments are in compliance with the national voluntary consensus standards for staffing, training, safe operations, personal protective equipment, and fitness; establishes a Task Force to Enhance Firefighter Safety to make recommendations to Congress on ways to increase compliance with firefighter safety standards.

H.R. 3791 also reauthorized the SAFER grant program at a level of $1.196 billion per year through FY2014. The legislation would have modified the SAFER grant program by shortening the grant period to three years, establishing a 20% local matching requirement for each year, removing the existing federal funding cap per hired firefighter, making national organizations eligible for recruitment and retention funds, and allowing DHS in the case of economic hardship to waive cost share requirements, the three-year grant period, and/or maintenance of expenditure requirements.

Senate Reauthorization Bill

On March 10, 2011, S. 550, the Fire Grants Authorization Act of 2011, was introduced by Senator Lieberman, Chairman of the Senate Committee on Homeland Security and Governmental Affairs. The Senate bill, while similar to the House bill, has a higher nonfederal match requirement for communities over 50K and higher match requirements for fire prevention and safety grants. Regarding SAFER, the Senate bill has a higher match requirement for hiring grants and would continue to require applicants to retain hired firefighters for at least one year after the grant expires (unless a waiver is obtained). On May 18, 2011, the Senate Committee on Homeland Security and Governmental Affairs ordered S. 550 to be reported with two amendments. One approved amendment is a requirement that the inspector general of DHS submit to Congress a report detailing whether and to what degree the grant programs are duplicative.

Table 2. Comparison of Selected Provisions in Fire Grant Reauthorization

Current Law (15 U.S.C. 2229 and 15 U.S.C. 2229a)	H.R. 2269 as introduced	S. 550 as reported
	Grant money allocation	
volunteer and combination fire departments shall receive a proportion of the total grant funding that is not less than the proportion of the U.S. population that those departments protect	25% to career fire departments	no less than 25% to career fire departments
	25% to volunteer fire departments	no less than 25% to volunteer fire departments
	25% to combination fire departments	no less than 25% to combination and paid-on-call fire departments
	10% competitive between career, volunteer, and combination departments	
5% (minimum) to fire prevention and safety grants	10% (minimum) to fire prevention and safety grants (includes fire safety research centers)	10% (minimum) to fire prevention and safety grants (includes fire safety research centers)
3.5% (minimum) to EMS provided by fire departments and nonaffiliated EMS organizations	2% (maximum) to volunteer non-fire service EMS	3.5% (minimum) to EMS provided by fire departments and nonaffiliated EMS organizations
2% (maximum) to nonaffiliated EMS organizations		2% (maximum) to nonaffiliated EMS organizations
	3% (maximum) to State fire training academies, no more than 1 grant and $1 million per state in a fiscal year	3% (maximum) to State training academies, no more than $1 million per state academy in any fiscal year
		Joint or Regional applications—two or more entities may submit an application to fund a joint or regional program or initiative, including acquisition of shared equipment or vehicles

Table 2. (Continued)

Current Law (15 U.S.C. 2229 and 15 U.S.C. 2229a)	H.R. 2269 as introduced	S. 550 as reported
	Grant recipient limits	
populations over 1 million—lesser of $2.75 million or 0.5% of total appropriation	$9 million—over 2.5m population	$9 million—over 2.5m population
	$6 million—1m to 2.5m population	$6 million—1m to 2.5m population
populations of 500K to 1 million—$1.75 million	$3 million—500K to 1m population	$3 million—500K to 1m population
	$2 million—100 to 500K population	$2 million—100 to 500K population
populations under 500K—$1 million	$1 million—under 100K population	$1 million—under 100K population
no single grant can exceed 0.5% of total funds appropriated for a single fiscal year		
DHS can waive the funding limits for populations up to 1 million in instances of extraordinary need; however the lesser of $2.75 million or 0.5% limit cannot be waived	DHS can waive funding limits for populations up to 2.5 million in instances of extraordinary need	FEMA may not award a grant exceeding 1% of all available grant funds, unless FEMA determines extraordinary need
	Nonfederal match requirements	
20% for populations over 50K	10% for populations over 20K	15% for populations over 50K
10% for populations 20K to 50K	5% for populations under 20K	10% for populations 20K to 50K
5% for populations less than 20K		5% for populations under 20K
No match requirement for non-fire department prevention and firefighter safety grants	No match requirement for all fire prevention and firefighter safety grants	5% match required for fire prevention and safety grants
	Maintenance of expenditures	
requires applicants to maintain expenditures at the same level as the average over the preceding two fiscal years	requires applicants to maintain expenditures at or above 80% of the average over the preceding two fiscal years	requires applicants to maintain expenditures at or above 80% of the average over the preceding two fiscal years

Current Law (15 U.S.C. 2229 and 15 U.S.C. 2229a)	H.R. 2269 as introduced	S. 550 as reported
	Economic hardship waivers	
no economic hardship waivers available	waivers available for nonfederal matching and maintenance of expenditures requirements, DHS will develop economic hardship waiver criteria in consultation with experts and interests representing the fire service and State and local governments	waivers available for nonfederal matching and maintenance of expenditures requirements, FEMA will develop economic hardship waiver guidelines considering unemployment rates, percentages of individuals eligible to receive food stamps, and other factors as appropriate.
	Authorizations	
FY2005—$900 million FY2006—$950 million FY2007—$1 billion FY2008—$1 billion FY2009—$1 billion	FY2012—$1 billion FY2013—$1 billion FY2014—$1 billion FY2015—$1 billion FY2016—$1 billion	FY2012—$950 million for each of FY2013 – FY2016, an amount equal to the amount authorized the previous fiscal year, increased by the percentage by which the Consumer Price Index for the previous fiscal year exceeds the preceding year. sunset: authority to award grants shall expire on October 1, 2016
	SAFER	
grant period is 4 years, grantees are required to retain for at least 1 year beyond the termination of their grants those firefighter positions hired under the grant	shortens the grant period to three years, grant recipients are required to retain for at least the entire 3 years of the grant period those firefighter positions hired under the grant	shortens the grant period to three years, grantees are required to retain for at least 1 year beyond the termination of their grants those firefighter positions hired under the grant
year 1—10% local match year 2—20% local match year 3—50% local match year 4—70% local match	establishes a 20% local matching requirement for each year	establishes a 25% local matching requirement for each year

Table 2. (Continued)

Current Law (15 U.S.C. 2229 and 15 U.S.C. 2229a)	H.R. 2269 as introduced	S. 550 as reported
total funding over 4 years for hiring a firefighter may not exceed $100K, adjusted annually for inflation	removes the existing federal funding cap per hired firefighter	the amount of funding provided for hiring a firefighter in any fiscal year may not exceed 75% of the usual annual cost of a first-year firefighter in that department
state, local, and Indian tribal governments eligible for recruitment and retention funds	additionally makes national organizations eligible for recruitment and retention funds allows DHS in the case of economic hardship to waive cost share requirements, the required retention period, the prohibition on supplanting local funds, and/or maintenance of expenditure requirements	additionally makes national organizations eligible for recruitment and retention funds allows DHS in the case of economic hardship to waive cost share requirements, the required retention period, the prohibition on supplanting local funds, and/or maintenance of expenditure requirements
authorized for 7 years starting at $1 billion in FY2004, ending at $1.194 billion in FY2010	reauthorizes the SAFER grant program FY2012 through FY2016 at a level of $1.194 billion per year	reauthorizes the SAFER grant program FY2012 through FY2016 at a level of $950 million per year, with each year adjusted for inflation
authority to make grants shall lapse 10 years from November 24, 2003	authority to make grants shall lapse 10 years after date of enactment	authority to award grants shall expire on October 1, 2016

Source: Compiled by CRS.

The other adopted amendment would sunset both AFG and SAFER grant programs on October 1, 2016, requiring the programs to subsequently be reauthorized past that date in order to continue.

Table 2 shows a comparison of selected provisions in S. 550 (as reported), H.R. 2269 (as introduced), and current law (15 U.S.C. 2229 and 15 U.S.C. 2229a).

Appropriations

From FY2001 through FY2003, the Assistance to Firefighters Grant (AFG) Program (as part of USFA/FEMA) received its primary appropriation through the VA-HUD-Independent Agencies Appropriation Act. In FY2004, the Assistance to Firefighters Program began to receive its annual appropriation through the House and Senate Appropriations Subcommittees on Homeland Security. Within the DHS/FEMA budget, the firefighter assistance account (which includes both AFG and SAFER) is located within State and Local Programs as part of the State and Regional Preparedness Program.

Table 3. Appropriations for Firefighter Assistance, FY2001-FY2012

	AFG	SAFER	SCGa	Total
FY2001	$100 million			$100 million
FY2002	$360 million			$360 million
FY2003	$745 million			$745 million
FY2004	$746 million			$746 million
FY2005	$650 million	$65 million		$715 million
FY2006	$539 million	$109 million		$648 million
FY2007	$547 million	$115 million		$662 million
FY2008	$560 million	$190 million		$750 million
FY2009	$565 million	$210 million	$210 million	$985 million
FY2010	$390 million	$420 million		$810 million
FY2011	$405 million	$405 million		$810 million
FY2012	$337.5 million	$337.5 million		$675 million
Total	$5.944 billion	$1.851 billion	$210 million	$8.005 billion

a. Assistance to Firefighters Fire Station Construction Grants (SCG) grants were funded by the American Recovery and Reinvestment Act (P.L. 111-5).

Table 4. Recent and Proposed Appropriations for Firefighter Assistance (millions of dollars)

	FY2010 (Admin. request)	FY2010 (P.L. 111-83)	FY2011 (Admin. request)	FY2011 (P.L. 112-10)	FY2012 (Admin. request)	FY2012 (P.L. 112-74)
FIRE						
Grants						
(AFG)	170	390	305	405	250	337.5
SAFER Grants	420	420	305	405	420	337.5
Total	590	810	610	810	670	675

The fire grant program is in its 11th year. Table 3 shows the appropriations history for firefighter assistance, including AFG, SAFER, and the Fire Station Construction Grants (SCG) provided in the American Recovery and Reinvestment Act (ARRA). Over $5.2 billion has been appropriated to the AFG program since FY2001, its initial year. Table 4 shows recent and proposed appropriated funding for the AFG and SAFER grant programs.

FY2010

For FY2010, the Obama administration proposed $170 million for AFG, a 70% decrease from the FY2009 level, and $420 million for SAFER, double the amount appropriated in FY2009. The total amount requested for firefighter assistance (AFG and SAFER) was $590 million, a 24% decrease from FY2009. The FY2010 budget proposal stated that the firefighter assistance grant process "will give priority to applications that enhance capabilities for terrorism response and other major incidents."[9]

The House FY2010 Department of Homeland Security appropriations bill (H.R. 2892; H.Rept. 111-157) provided $800 million for firefighter assistance, including $380 million for AFG and $420 million for SAFER. Although the SAFER level matched the administration's request, the AFG level was more than twice what the administration proposed. According to the committee report, the administration's request of $170 million for AFG "is woefully inadequate given the vast needs of fire departments across the nation for equipment." The committee directed FEMA to continue granting funds to local fire departments, include the United States Fire Administration in the grant decision process, and maintain an all-hazard focus while prohibiting the limiting of eligible activities including wellness.

The House passed H.R. 2892 on June 24, 2009. During floor consideration of H.R. 2892, the House approved a manager's amendment that added $10 million to the AFG account. Therefore, the House-passed total for AFG was $390 million.

The Senate FY2010 Department of Homeland Security appropriations bill (S. 1298; S.Rept. 111- 31) provided $800 million for firefighter assistance, including $380 million for AFG and $420 million for SAFER. The Appropriations Committee directed DHS to continue funding applications according to local priorities and priorities established by the United States Fire Administration, and to continue direct funding to fire departments and the peer review process.

The Senate passed H.R. 2892 on July 9, 2009. During floor consideration, the Senate adopted an amendment (S.Amdt. 1458) that added $10 million to the AFG account. Therefore, the Senate-passed total for AFG was also $390 million.

The conference report for the Department of Homeland Security Appropriations Act, 2010 (H.Rept. 111-298) was passed by the House on October 15. H.Rept. 111-298 provided $390 million for AFG and $420 million for SAFER, identical to the levels in both the House- and Senate-passed H.R. 2892. The conferees directed FEMA to continue the present practice of funding applications according to local priorities and those established by the USFA, to maintain an all-hazards focus, to grant funds for eligible activities in accordance with the authorizing statute, and to continue the current grant application and review process as specified in the House report. The conference report was passed by the House on October 15, by the Senate on October 20, and signed into law, P.L. 111-83, on October 28, 2009.

FY2011

The administration's FY2011 budget proposed $305 million for AFG (a 22% decrease from the FY2010 level) and $305 million for SAFER (a 27% decrease). The total amount requested for firefighter assistance (AFG and SAFER) was $610 million, a 25% decrease from FY2010. The FY2011 budget proposal stated that the firefighter assistance grant process "will give priority to applications that enhance capabilities for terrorism response and other major incidents."[10]

On June 24, 2010, the House Subcommittee on Homeland Security Appropriations approved $840 million for firefighter assistance, including $420 million for AFG and $420 million for SAFER.

On July 19, 2010, the Senate Appropriations Committee approved $810 million for firefighter assistance (including $390 million for AFG and $420 million for SAFER), the same level as FY2010 and 33% more than the administration proposal. In the bill report (S.Rept. 111-222), the committee directed DHS to continue funding applications according to local priorities and priorities established by the United States Fire Administration, and to continue direct funding to fire departments and the peer review process. The committee also directed FEMA to submit the U.S. Fire Service Needs Assessment, and to brief the committee regarding the implementation of the recommendations of the recent GAO report (GAO-10-64) on additional actions which would improve the grants process.

H.R. 1, the Full-Year Continuing Appropriations Act, 2011, as introduced on February 11, 2011, would have provided $300 million to AFG and zero funding for SAFER. However, on February 16, 2011, H.Amdt. 223 (offered by Representative Pascrell and agreed to by the House by a vote of 318-113) restored AFG to $390 million and SAFER to $420 million (the FY2010 levels). H.R. 1 was passed by the House on February 18, 2011. S.Amdt. 149 to H.R. 1—which was rejected by the full Senate on March 9, 2011—would have funded AFG at $405 million and SAFER at $405 million.

Subsequently, the full-year continuing appropriation bill for FY2011, which was signed into law on April 15, 2011 (Department of Defense and Continuing Appropriations Act, 2011, P.L. 112-10) funded AFG at $405 million and SAFER at $405 million for FY2011. P.L. 112-10 also contained language that removes FY2011 SAFER cost-share requirements and allows SAFER grants to be used to rehire laid-off firefighters and fill positions eliminated through attrition. However, P.L. 112-10 did not remove the requirement that SAFER grants fund a firefighter position for four years, with the fifth year funded wholly by the grant recipient. The law also did not waive the cap of $100K per firefighter hired by a SAFER grant.

FY2012

The administration's FY2012 budget proposed $670 million for firefighter assistance, including $250 million for AFG and $420 million for SAFER. According to the budget proposal, the request would fund 2,200 firefighter positions and approximately 5,000 AFG grants. The FY2012 budget proposal stated that the firefighter assistance grant process "will give priority to applications that enhance capabilities for terrorism response and other major incidents."[11]

The Department of Homeland Security Appropriations, 2012, bill (H.R. 2017) was reported by the House Appropriations Committee on May 26, 2011. The House Committee bill would have provided $350 million for firefighter assistance, including $200 million for AFG and $150 million for SAFER. The

House Appropriations bill report (H.Rept. 112-91) directed FEMA to continue granting funds directly to local fire departments and to include the United States Fire Administration during the grant decision process. FEMA was also directed to maintain an all-hazards focus and was prohibited from limiting beyond current law the list of eligible activities, including those related to wellness.

During the House floor consideration of H.R. 2017, two firefighter assistance amendments were adopted. The first amendment (offered by Mr. LaTourette and Mr. Pascrell, and agreed to by a recorded vote of 333-87) raised FY2012 funding levels to $335 million for AFG and $335 million for SAFER. The total level for firefighter assistance ($670 million) is equal to the level requested by the administration.

The second amendment (offered by Mr. Price of North Carolina and agreed to by a recorded vote of 264-157) prohibited enforcement of various SAFER requirements for grantees. These waivers would allow FY2012 SAFER grants to be used to rehire laid-off firefighters and fill positions eliminated through attrition, remove cost-share requirements, allow grants to extend longer than the current five year duration, and permit the amount of funding per position at levels exceeding the current limit of $100,000.

The Department of Homeland Security Appropriations, 2012, bill (H.R. 2017) was passed by the House on June 2, 2011.

On September 7, 2011, the Senate Appropriations Committee approved $750 million for firefighter assistance in FY2012 (S.Rept. 112-74), which is a 12% increase over the House-passed level. The total included $375 million for AFG and $375 million for SAFER. As does the House bill, the Senate bill also waived or prohibited SAFER requirements in FY2012.

P.L. 112-74, the Consolidated Appropriations Act, FY2012, provided $675 million for firefighter assistance, including $337.5 million for AFG and $337.5 million for SAFER. The conference report directed FEMA to continue funding applications according to local priorities and those established by the USFA, to maintain an all hazards focus, and to continue the current grant application and review process as specified in the House report.

FIRE STATION CONSTRUCTION GRANTS IN THE ARRA

Since its inception, the traditional fire grant program has provided money specifically for health and safety related modifications of fire stations, but has not funded major upgrades, renovations, or construction. The American

Recovery and Reinvestment Act (ARRA) of 2009 (P.L. 111-5) provided an additional $210 million in firefighter assistance grants for modifying, upgrading, or constructing state and local non-federal fire stations, provided that 5% be set aside for program administration and provided that no grant shall exceed $15 million. The conference report (H.Rept. 111-16) cited DHS estimates that this spending would create 2,000 jobs. The ARRA also included a provision (§603) that waived the matching requirement for SAFER grants funded by appropriations in FY2009 and FY2010.

The application period for ARRA Assistance to Firefighters Fire Station Construction Grants (SCG) opened on June 11 and closed on July 10, 2009. There is no cost share requirement for SCG grants. Eligible applicants are non-federal fire departments that provide fire protection services to local communities. Ineligible applicants include federal fire departments, EMS or rescue organizations, airport fire departments, for-profit fire departments, fire training centers, emergency communications centers, auxiliaries and fire service organizations or associations, and search and rescue teams or similar organizations without fire suppression responsibilities.

DHS/FEMA received 6,025 SCG applications for $9.9 billion in federal funds.[12] As of October 1, 2010, 119 SCG grants were awarded, totaling $207.461 million to fire departments within the United States. A complete list of SCG awards is available at http://www.firegrantsupport.com/ content/html /scg/Awards09.aspx/.

On February 15, 2011, the Firefighting Investment, Renewal, and Employment Act or FIRE Act (H.R. 716) was introduced to authorize $210 million for each of fiscal years 2012 through 2016 for competitive grants for modifying, upgrading, or constructing nonfederal fire stations.

SAFER GRANTS

In response to concerns over the adequacy of firefighter staffing, the 108th Congress enacted the Staffing for Adequate Fire and Emergency Response (SAFER) Act as Section 1057 of the FY2004 National Defense Authorization Act (P.L. 108-136; signed into law November 24, 2003). The SAFER grant program is codified as Section 34 of the Federal Fire Prevention and Control Act of 1974 (15 U.S.C. 2229a). The SAFER Act authorizes grants to career, volunteer, and combination fire departments for the purpose of increasing the number of firefighters to help communities meet industry minimum standards and attain 24-hour staffing to provide adequate protection from fire and fire-related hazards. Also authorized are grants to volunteer fire departments for activities related to the recruitment and retention of volunteers. P.L. 108-136 authorizes over one billion dollars per year through FY2010 for SAFER.

Two types of grants are authorized by the SAFER Act: hiring grants and recruitment and retention grants. *Hiring grants* cover a four-year term and are cost shared with the local jurisdiction. According to the statute, the federal share shall not exceed 90% in the first year of the grant, 80% in the second year, 50% in the third year, and 30% in the fourth year. The grantee must commit to retaining the firefighter or firefighters hired with the SAFER grant for at least one additional year after the federal money expires. Total federal funding for hiring a firefighter over the four-year grant period may not exceed $100,000, although that total may be adjusted for inflation. While the majority of hiring grants will be awarded to career and combination fire departments, the SAFER Act specifies that 10% of the total SAFER appropriation be awarded to volunteer or majority-volunteer departments for the hiring of personnel.

Additionally, at least 10% of the total SAFER appropriation is set aside for *recruitment and retention grants*, which are available to volunteer and combination fire departments for activities related to the recruitment and retention of volunteer firefighters. Also eligible for recruitment and retention grants are local and statewide organizations that represent the interests of volunteer firefighters. No local cost sharing is required for recruitment and retention grants.

For more information on the SAFER program, see CRS Report RL33375, *Staffing for Adequate Fire and Emergency Response: The SAFER Grant Program*, by Lennard G. Kruger.

PROGRAM EVALUATION

On May 13, 2003, the U.S. Fire Administration (USFA) released the first independent evaluation of the Assistance to Firefighters Program. Conducted by the U.S. Department of Agriculture's Leadership Development Academy Executive Potential Program, the survey study presented a number of recommendations and concluded overall that the program was "highly effective in improving the readiness and capabilities of firefighters across the nation."[13] Another evaluation of the fire grant program was released by the DHS Office of Inspector General in September 2003. The report concluded that the program "succeeded in achieving a balanced distribution of funding through a competitive grant process,"[14] and made a number of specific recommendations for improving the program.

At the request of DHS, the National Academy of Public Administration conducted a study to help identify potential new strategic directions for the Assistance to Firefighters Grant program and to provide advice on how to effectively plan, manage, and measure program accomplishments. Released in April 2007, the report recommended consideration of new strategic directions related to national preparedness, prevention vs. response, social equity, regional cooperation, and emergency medical response. According to the report, the "challenge for the AFG program will be to support a gradual shift in direction without losing major strengths of its current management approach—including industry driven priority setting and its well-respected peer review process."[15]

The Consolidated Appropriations Act of 2008 (P.L. 110-161), in the accompanying Joint Explanatory Statement, directed the Government Accountability Office (GAO) to review the application and award process for fire and SAFER grants. Additionally, FEMA was directed to peer review grant applications that best address the program's priorities and criteria as established by FEMA and the fire service. Those criteria necessary for peer-review must be included in the grant application package. Applicants whose grant applications are not reviewed must receive an official notification detailing why the application did not meet the criteria for review. Applications must be rank-ordered, and funded following the rank order.

In October 2009, GAO sent a report to Congress finding that FEMA has met most statutory requirements for awarding fire grants.[16] GAO recommended that FEMA establish a procedure to track EMS awards, ensure that grant priorities are better aligned with application questions and scoring values, and provide specific feedback to rejected applicants.

In June 2011, the National Fire Protection Association (NFPA) released its *Third Needs Assessment of the U.S. Fire Service*, which seeks to identify gaps and needs in the fire service, and measures the impact that fire grants have had on filling those gaps and needs. According to the study:

> Needs have declined to a considerable degree in a number of areas, particularly personal protective and firefighting equipment, two types of resource that received the largest shares of funding from the Assistance to Firefighters grants (AFG). Declines in needs have been more modest in some other important areas, such as training, which have received much smaller shares of AFG grant funds.[17]

DISTRIBUTION OF FIRE GRANTS

The FIRE Act statute prescribes 14 different purposes for which fire grant money *may* be used (see 15 U.S.C. 2229(b)(3)). These are: hiring firefighters; training firefighters; creating rapid intervention teams; certifying fire inspectors; establishing wellness and fitness programs; funding emergency medical services; acquiring firefighting vehicles; acquiring firefighting equipment; acquiring personal protective equipment; modifying fire stations for health and safety; enforcing fire codes; funding fire prevention programs; educating the public about arson prevention and detection; and providing incentives for the recruitment and retention of volunteer firefighters. The DHS has the discretion to decide which of those purposes will be funded for a given grant year. Since the program commenced in FY2001, the majority of fire grant funding has been used by fire departments to purchase firefighting equipment, personal protective equipment, and firefighting vehicles.

Eligible applicants are limited primarily to fire departments (defined as an agency or organization that has a formally recognized arrangement with a state, local, or tribal authority to provide fire suppression, fire prevention and rescue services to a population within a fixed geographical area). Emergency Medical Services (EMS) activities are eligible for fire grants, including a limited number (no more than 2% of funds allocated) to EMS organizations not affiliated with hospitals. Additionally, a separate competition is held for fire prevention and firefighter safety research and development grants, which are available to national, state, local, or community fire prevention or safety organizations (including, but not limited to, fire departments). For official program guidelines, frequently-asked-questions, the latest awards announcements, and other information, see the Assistance to Firefighters Grant program web page at http://www.firegrantsupport.com/.

The FIRE Act statute provides overall guidelines on how fire grant money will be distributed and administered. The law directs that volunteer and combination departments receive a proportion of the total grant funding that is not less than the proportion of the U.S. population that those departments protect (34% for combination, 21% for all-volunteer). The Assistance to Firefighters Grant Program Reauthorization Act of 2004 (Title XXXVI of P.L. 108-375) raised award caps and lowered nonfederal matching requirements (based on recipient community population), extended eligibility to nonaffiliated emergency medical services (i.e., ambulance services not affiliated with fire departments), and expanded the scope of grants to include firefighter safety R&D.

There is no set geographical formula for the distribution of fire grants—fire departments throughout the nation apply, and award decisions are made by a peer panel based on the merits of the application and the needs of the community. However, the law does require that fire grants should be distributed to a diverse mix of fire departments, with respect to type of department (paid, volunteer, or combination), geographic location, and type of community served (e.g., urban, suburban, or rural).[18] The Fire Act's implementing regulation provides that

> In a few cases, to fulfill our obligations under the law to make grants to a variety of departments, we may also make funding decisions using rank order as the preliminary basis, and then analyze the type of fire department (paid, volunteer, or combination fire departments), the size and character of the community it serves (urban, suburban, or rural), and/or the geographic location of the fire department. In these instances where we are making decisions based on geographic location, we will use States as the basic geographic unit.[19]

According to the FY2011 Program Guidance for the Assistance to Firefighters Program, career (paid) departments will compete against other career departments for up to 47% of the available funding, while volunteer and combination departments will compete for at least 53% of the available funding.[20] However, given that less than 10% of fire grant applications are historically received from career departments, funding levels are likely not to reach the 47% ceiling for career departments. Additionally, each fire department that applies is classified as either urban, suburban, or rural. In FY2006, 4.3% of the total number of fire grant awards went to urban areas, 17.8% to suburban areas, and 77.7% to rural areas. Of the total amount of federal funding awarded, 7.7% went to urban areas, 18.2% to suburban areas, and 73.9% to rural areas.[21]

Finally, in an effort to maximize the diversity of awardees, the geographic location of an applicant (using states as the basic geographic unit) is used as a deciding factor in cases where applicants have similar qualifications. Table 5 shows a state-by-state breakdown of fire grant funding for FY2001 through FY2010, while Table 6 shows a state-by-state breakdown of SAFER grant funding for FY2005 through FY2010. Table 7 provides an in-depth look at the FY2009 fire grants, showing, for each state, the number of fire departments in each state,[22] the number of fire grant applications, the total amount requested, the total amount awarded, and the amount of funds awarded as a percentage of funds requested.

Table 5. State-by-State Distribution of Fire Grants, FY2001-FY2010 (millions of dollars)

	FY01	FY02	FY03	FY04	FY05	FY06	FY07	FY08	FY09	FY10	Total
AL	3.085	12.503	23.329	25.097	20.836	22.027	19.903	23.332	19.966	14.591	184.669
AK	1.303	2.641	5.242	2.522	3.111	0.754	2.454	0.990	0.935	0.568	20.52
AZ	1.37	3.6	7.490	9.808	7.905	4.041	4.932	5.440	4.716	2.873	52.175
AR	1.337	4.635	10.675	13.680	10.402	7.699	7.799	7.107	8.174	5.111	76.619
CA	5.905	18.978	30.060	29.793	25.631	17.856	18.730	26.198	23.644	21.860	218.655
CO	1.003	3.968	6.168	5.585	6.073	3.213	4.742	2.490	6.11	3.369	42.721
CT	1.828	4.675	10.841	9.991	7.287	5.479	6.630	6.925	5.231	3.166	62.053
DE	0.132	0.372	1.096	1.755	1.161	1.107	0.518	0.231	1.251	0.282	7.905
DC	0	0.22	0	0	0.453	0	0.376	1.171	0	0.368	2.588
FL	2.865	10.16	16.344	15.969	17.922	6.787	8.288	6.738	12.581	12.557	110.211
GA	2.375	6.079	13.791	11.857	10.168	8.887	9.068	7.959	8.981	6.192	85.357
HI	0	1.182	0.947	0.864	1.205	0.264	0.436	0.772	0.609	0.261	6.54
ID	0.916	2.744	6.001	4.828	4.684	2.712	4.297	2.687	2.883	2.361	34.113
IL	2.417	13.398	28.810	27.238	25.433	21.120	21.923	21.325	25.24	14.809	201.713
IN	2.703	8.739	20.456	18.646	15.779	14.447	13.831	13.092	15.179	10.759	133.631
IA	1.301	7.284	16.087	16.430	13.119	10.064	9.298	9.877	9.695	5.818	98.973
KS	1.153	5.118	10.850	10.211	7.165	4.984	5.502	3.928	6.682	3.055	58.648
KY	2.215	7.896	19.832	16.150	14.215	13.308	13.081	17.153	13.108	8.081	125.039
LA	3.344	10.084	12.248	11.101	11.630	6.935	5.473	7.033	8.073	4.414	80.335
ME	1.296	4.319	10.323	10.031	6.124	6.702	5.486	4.904	3.462	1.348	53.995
MD	0.739	4.08	8.153	10.227	8.771	10.368	7.712	5.525	5.221	4.545	65.341
MA	2.301	8.386	15.715	13.958	13.529	8.957	11.644	9.532	11.957	8.083	104.062
MI	2.815	8.948	17.247	20.005	15.088	15.798	15.399	15.482	18.045	9.502	138.329
MN	2.133	8.149	17.510	18.609	14.894	14.718	16.600	13.082	17.253	18.923	141.871

Table 5. (Continued)

	FY01	FY02	FY03	FY04	FY05	FY06	FY07	FY08	FY09	FY10	Total
MS	1.763	6.755	15.679	11.329	9.856	7.885	8.052	7.761	8.436	5.66	83.176
MO	3.079	10.291	19.573	17.757	14.246	13.202	10.611	11.589	12.973	9.21	122.531
MT	1.164	3.726	8.361	7.271	6.656	5.839	7.330	4.670	5.179	3.204	53.4
NE	1.034	2.392	7.820	6.577	5.116	4.399	4.443	4.324	4.341	0.441	40.887
NV	0.282	1.446	3.312	1.405	1.946	0.857	1.530	0.687	0.855	1.437	13.757
NH	0.594	1.887	4.584	5.694	4.563	3.307	3.219	2.723	2.834	1.496	30.901
NJ	2.596	6.339	19.982	16.488	14.691	12.386	13.266	13.201	15.502	9.687	124.138
NM	1.455	3.463	5.048	3.653	2.259	1.461	1.367	1.101	1.605	1.632	23.044
NY	3.978	14.728	34.320	35.030	36.009	33.804	22.664	30.204	23.235	13.367	247.339
NC	1.949	10.239	22.864	22.360	19.315	18.309	20.031	18.460	20.881	13.137	167.545
ND	0.546	2.613	5.105	3.391	2.673	2.459	3.100	3.297	2.527	1.594	27.305
OH	2.731	13.742	26.997	29.107	27.344	25.380	26.433	26.938	33.164	20.386	232.222
OK	1.864	4.939	10.540	10.393	8.757	10.852	7.220	6.875	7.239	3.527	72.206
OR	1.596	4.892	9.896	10.122	10.014	9.288	5.943	8.438	5.986	6.332	72.507
PA	2.89	16.97	45.179	47.898	39.233	41.259	43.610	41.041	37.231	19.677	334.988
RI	0.407	1.507	2.327	1.917	2.129	2.025	0.855	1.395	2.46	1.533	16.555
SC	1.554	5.257	11.832	14.150	10.544	8.028	10.470	11.040	11.227	8.684	92.786
SD	0.904	3.142	5.602	4.693	3.570	2.989	2.474	2.069	2.527	0.753	28.723
TN	2.46	11.509	19.306	18.686	15.047	11.209	12.955	16.074	13.311	11.259	131.816
TX	3.697	15.644	29.264	30.118	23.480	18.035	17.691	20.458	19.469	9.941	187.797
UT	0.9	2.754	4.628	3.880	2.188	2.213	3.378	0.934	2.295	2.985	26.155
VT	0.451	1.971	5.163	4.747	2.071	1.456	1.820	1.046	1.974	0.689	21.388
VA	2.066	8.79	15.816	16.668	14.357	8.317	10.403	8.370	6.405	5.991	97.183
WA	1.535	7.544	18.808	19.565	15.763	16.150	12.951	13.050	10.064	7.961	123.391

	FY01	FY02	FY03	FY04	FY05	FY06	FY07	FY08	FY09	FY10	Total
WV	1.067	3.966	9.942	9.133	10.143	5.838	7.164	7.238	5.331	5.074	64.896
WI	2.077	7.518	18.234	19.668	17.685	13.994	19.439	15.216	15.17	9.569	138.57
WY	1.09	1.612	3.507	1.811	2.032	1.197	1.645	1.023	1.427	0.086	15.43
PR	0.657	0.382	1.643	1.140	1.104	0.528	0.019	0.074	1.154	0	6.701
MP	0.145	0.225	0	0	0.220	0.172	0	0	0	0.7	1.462
GU	0	0.016		0	0	0.287	0	0	0	0	0.303
AS	0.164	0	0	0.284	0	0	0	0	0	0	0.448
VI	0.741	0	0.544	0	0	0	0	0.233	0	0	1.518
	91.97	334.41	695.12	679.30	585.61	491.37	494.22	492.52	503.25	338.91	4706

Source: Department of Homeland Security. Current as of October 7, 2011.

Table 6. State-by-State Distribution of SAFER Grants, FY2005-FY2010, (millions of dollars)

	FY2005	FY2006	FY2007	FY2008	FY2009	FY2010	Total
Alabama	1.611	6.215	4.236	7.314	4.288	8.531	32.195
Alaska	1.051	0.205	0.418	1.438	0.328	6.072	9.512
Arizona	1.560	3.559	4.428	6.613	6.768	10.357	33.285
Arkansas	0.394	1.820	0.377	3.834	0.976	2.206	9.607
California	5.221	5.212	4.259	4.212	31.501	63.13	113.535
Colorado	1.584	3.479	1.730	2.02	0.955	3.384	13.152
Connecticut	0.130	0.191	0.856	3.92	2.214	3.496	10.807
Delaware	0	0.135	0	0.398	0	1.723	2.256
District of Columbia	0	0	0	0	0	0	0
Florida	6.576	9.329	6.217	17.185	24.105	17.721	81.133
Georgia	5.354	2.085	2.842	17.438	4.844	10.384	42.947
Hawaii	0	0	0	1.626	0	0.1	1.726

Table 6. (Continued)

	FY2005	FY2006	FY2007	FY2008	FY2009	FY2010	Total
Idaho	0.063	0.621	0.626	0.774	1.336	2.897	6.317
Illinois	1.340	4.463	9.933	5.85	2.496	10.848	34.93
Indiana	0	0.099	2.687	4.577	8.295	9.931	25.589
Iowa	0.169	0.144	0.980	1.288	1.045	0.081	3.707
Kansas	0.667	0.045	1.029	1.872	2.806	2.285	8.704
Kentucky	0.152	2.890	0.429	2.466	0.338	0.893	7.168
Louisiana	3.430	3.078	4.728	8.62	10.515	0.182	30.553
Maine	0.081	0	0.316	0.951	0.739	1.047	3.134
Maryland	0.096	1.862	1.526	3.171	4.429	2.145	13.229
Massachusetts	1.300	2.079	4.372	2.690	18.385	34.422	63.248
Michigan	1.759	0.592	0	0.628	13.286	22.493	38.758
Minnesota	0.300	1.089	0.375	3.246	1.256	0.789	7.055
Mississippi	0.756	0.594	0.115	1.608	0	1.209	4.282
Missouri	1.467	3.547	4.551	2.381	1.474	5.618	19.038
Montana	0.034	0.255	2.635	2.955	0.458	0.973	7.31
Nebraska	0	0.873	0.632	1.951	0.802	0.493	4.751
Nevada	1.500	1.714	0.632	0.086	0.577	2.459	6.968
New Hampshire	0.400	1.035	1.528	0.225	0	0.353	3.541
New Jersey	6.374	3.971	2.953	4.389	0.556	56.648	74.891
New Mexico	0	3.123	1.309	0.108	0.499	1.854	6.893
New York	1.540	2.991	2.845	4.412	8.227	18.239	38.254
North Carolina	2.155	5.533	5.371	18.183	2.256	6.375	39.873
North Dakota	0	0.609	0	1.518	1.517	2.139	5.783
Ohio	1.319	1.881	2.255	3.737	29.606	21.04	59.838

	FY2005	FY2006	FY2007	FY2008	FY2009	FY2010	Total
Oklahoma	0.147	0.699	0.531	2.782	0	9.127	13.286
Oregon	1.710	2.141	2.649	2.071	0.677	6.166	15.414
Pennsylvania	1.244	1.475	2.633	3.515	1.176	7.926	17.969
Rhode Island	0.400	0	0.105	0	1.561	4.249	6.315
South Carolina	0.456	0.863	3.218	8.158	2.41	2.064	17.169
South Dakota	0.063	0.311	0.211	0.552	0	0.648	1.785
Tennessee	2.700	2.719	3.683	1.856	1.148	7.374	19.48
Texas	0.951	10.961	8.779	19.06	3.158	12.65	55.559
Utah	0.900	3.312	2.098	3.955	1.824	4.583	16.672
Vermont	0	0.621	0.632	0	0.119	0	1.372
Virginia	2.091	3.554	0.782	1.849	4.891	8.995	22.162
Washington	2.298	2.897	7.340	9.476	2.847	13.779	38.637
West Virginia	0	0.187	0.681	0.16	0.287	0.398	1.713
Wisconsin	0	0.072	1.223	4.502	0	0.12	5.917
Wyoming	0	0	0.316	2.329	0.263	0.997	3.905
Puerto Rico	0	0	0	0	0	0	0
Northern Mariana Islands	0	0	0	0	0	1.404	1.404
Marshall Islands	0	0	0	0	0	0	0
Guam	0	0	0	0	0	0	0
American Samoa	0	0	0	0	0	0	0
Virgin Islands	0	0	0	0	0	0	0
Republic of Palau	0	0	0	0	0	0	0
Total	61.356	105.142	113.665	203.964	207.258	413.017	1104.402

Source: Department of Homeland Security. Current as of October 7, 2011.

Table 7. Requests and Awards for Fire Grant Funding, FY2009

State	Number of fire/EMS departments	Number of applications	Federal funds requested ($millions)	Federal funds awarded ($millions)	Funds awarded as a % of funds requested
Alabama	966	779	114.977	19.966	17.37%
Alaska	75	56	11.088	0.935	8.43%
Arizona	283	178	33.907	4.716	13.91%
Arkansas	826	420	51.329	8.174	15.92%
California	823	534	118.658	23.644	19.93%
Colorado	375	166	32.238	6.11	18.95%
Connecticut	401	253	42.249	5.231	12.38%
Delaware	77	34	5.219	1.251	23.97%
District of Columbia	18	1	2.777	0	0.00%
Florida	755	289	69.808	12.581	18.02%
Georgia	799	395	64.942	8.981	13.83%
Hawaii	20	3	0.867	0.609	70.24%
Idaho	212	116	17.805	2.883	16.19%
Illinois	1090	885	135.105	25.24	18.68%
Indiana	670	507	78.287	15.179	19.39%
Iowa	864	560	60.512	9.695	16.02%
Kansas	680	276	33.304	6.682	20.06%
Kentucky	796	630	89.445	13.108	14.65%
Louisiana	557	262	43.072	8.073	18.74%
Maine	431	307	38.283	3.462	9.04%
Maryland	418	205	32.181	5.221	16.22%
Massachusetts	408	349	68.931	11.957	17.35%
Michigan	865	776	114.942	18.045	15.70%

State	Number of fire/EMS departments	Number of applications	Federal funds requested ($millions)	Federal funds awarded ($millions)	Funds awarded as a % of funds requested
Minnesota	770	521	75.941	17.253	22.72%
Mississippi	756	435	57.183	8.436	14.75%
Missouri	865	520	77.004	12.973	16.85%
Montana	283	193	29.121	5.179	17.78%
Nebraska	486	180	22.743	4.341	19.09%
Nevada	161	32	6.162	0.855	13.88%
New Hampshire	256	145	25.849	2.834	10.96%
New Jersey	1044	618	93.849	15.502	16.52%
New Mexico	341	91	20.932	1.605	7.67%
New York	1894	1315	175.848	23.235	13.21%
North Carolina	1411	728	122.919	20.881	16.99%
North Dakota	322	153	16.141	2.527	15.66%
Ohio	1338	1062	155.248	33.164	21.36%
Oklahoma	772	397	51.534	7.239	14.05%
Oregon	360	231	36.695	5.986	16.31%
Pennsylvania	2635	2255	296.739	37.231	12.55%
Rhode Island	101	74	14.173	2.46	17.36%
South Carolina	592	419	67.334	11.227	16.67%
South Dakota	345	179	21.155	2.527	11.95%
Tennessee	649	660	96.677	13.311	13.77%
Texas	1883	775	137.322	19.469	14.18%
Utah	221	120	14.46	2.295	15.87%
Vermont	255	104	10.377	1.974	19.02%
Virginia	822	327	59.621	6.405	10.74%
Washington	543	357	63.019	10.064	15.97%

Table 7. (Continued)

State	Number of fire/EMS departments	Number of applications	Federal funds requested ($millions)	Federal funds awarded ($millions)	Funds awarded as a % of funds requested
West Virginia	476	365	49.557	5.331	10.76%
Wisconsin	901	713	92.114	15.17	16.47%
Wyoming	135	51	7.748	1.427	18.42%
Puerto Rico	7	8	8.233	1.154	14.02%
Northern Marianas	Not available	2	0.268	0	0.00%
Virgin Islands	Not available	2	0.565	0	0.00%
Guam	Not available	2	1.524	0	0.00%
Total	30,185	21,015	3167.966	503.253	15.89%

Sources: Department of Homeland Security and firehouse.com (number of firehouse/EMS departments, updated June 2009).

As Table 7 shows, the entire pool of fire department applicants received about 16% of the funds they requested in FY2009. This compares to 15% in FY2008, 16% in FY2007, 21% in FY2006, 22% in FY2005, 28% in FY2004, and 34% in FY2003. The downward trend reflects the fact that the number of applications and federal funds requested have trended upward over these years, while appropriations for the fire grant program have declined over the same period.

ISSUES IN THE 112TH CONGRESS

Because the 111th Congress did not enact the Fire Grants Reauthorization Act, the 112th Congress may revisit the issue, and may consider whether and how to modify the reauthorization bills. On March 10, 2011, S. 550, the Fire Grants Authorization Act of 2011, was introduced; on May 18, 2011, S. 550 was ordered to be reported by the Committee. On June 22, 2011, a House version of the Fire Grants Reauthorization Act of 2011 (H.R. 2269) was introduced. Debate over the AFG reauthorization has reflected a competition for funding between career/urban/suburban departments and volunteer/rural departments. The urgency of this debate could be heightened by possible reductions of overall AFG funding and the economic downturn in many local communities increasingly hard pressed to allocate funding for their local fire departments.

Meanwhile, the Second Session of the 112th Congress will consider the administration's FY2013 request for AFG and SAFER. As is the case with many federal programs, concerns in the 112th Congress over the federal budget deficit could impact budget levels for AFG and SAFER. At the same time, firefighter assistance budgets will likely receive heightened scrutiny from the fire community, given the national economic downturn and local budgetary cutbacks that many fire departments are now facing.

End Notes

[1] For a list of federal programs providing assistance to state and local first responders, see CRS Report R40246, *Department of Homeland Security Assistance to States and Localities: A Summary and Issues for the 111th Congress*, by Shawn Reese.

[2] "Firefighter assistance" is codified as §33 of the Federal Fire Prevention and Control Act (15 U.S.C. 2229).

[3] See http://science.house.gov/publications/hearings_markups_details.aspx?NewsID=2539.

[4] According to the National Fire Protection Association (NFPA), there are an estimated 30,185 fire departments in the United States (2007 data). Of those, 7.5% are career departments, 5.8% are mostly career, 16.5% are mostly volunteer, and 70.1% are all volunteer. Most career firefighters (74%) are in communities that protect 25,000 or more people, while most volunteer firefighters (95%) are in departments that protect fewer than 25,000, and more than half are located in small, rural departments that protect fewer than 2,500 people.

[5] Kevin O'Connor, Assistant to the General President, International Association of Fire Fighters, testimony before the House Subcommittee on Technology and Innovation, Committee on Science and Technology, July 8, 2009, p. 3, http://gop.science.house.gov/Media /hearings/ets09/july8/oconnor.pdf.

[6] Ibid.

[7] Jack Carriger, First Vice Chairman of the National Volunteer Fire Council, testimony before the House Subcommittee on Technology and Innovation, Committee on Science and Technology, July 8, 2009, p. 3, http://democrats.science.house.gov/Media /file/Commdocs /hearings/2009/Tech/8jul/Carriger_Testimony.pdf.

[8] Ibid.

[9] Office of Management and Budget, Appendix: Budget of the United States Government, FY2010, p. 547.

[10] Office of Management and Budget, Appendix: Budget of the United States Government, FY2011, p. 557.

[11] Office of Management and Budget, Appendix: Budget of the United States Government, FY2012, p. 538.

[12] Detailed SCG application statistics are available at http://www.firegrantsupport.com/docs/2009 AFSCGAppStats.pdf.

[13] For full report see http://www.usfa.fema.gov/downloads/pdf/affgp-fy01-usda-report.pdf.

[14] Department of Homeland Security, Office of Inspections, Evaluations, and Special Reviews, "A Review of the Assistance to Firefighters Grant Program," OIG-ISP-01-03, September 2003, p. 3. Available at http://www.dhs.gov/ xoig/assets/mgmtrpts/OIG_ Review_Fire_ Assist.pdf.

[15] National Academy of Public Administration, *Assistance to Firefighters Grant Program: Assessing Performance*, April 2007, p. xvii. Available at http://www.napawash.org/pc_ management_studies/ Fire_Grants_Report_April2007.pdf.

[16] U.S. Government Accountability Office, *Fire Grants: FEMA Has Met Most Requirements for Awarding Fire Grants, but Additional Actions Would Improve Its Grant Process*, GAO-10-64, October 2009, http://www.gao.gov/ new.items/d1064.pdf.

[17] National Fire Protection Association, *Third Needs Assessment of the U.S. Fire Service*, June 2011, abstract. available at http://www.nfpa.org/assets/files//2011NeedsAssessment.pdf.

[18] 15 U.S.C. 2229(b)(9).

[19] 44 CFR Part 152.6(c).

[20] For the FY2011 round of awards, no less than 33.5% of AFG funds must be awarded to combination departments, and no less than 19.5% of AFG funds must be awarded to all-volunteer departments. See Department of Homeland Security, *Assistance to Firefighters Grants, Guidance and Application Kit,* Section I, August 2011, p. 41.

[21] Department of Homeland Security, Grant Programs Directorate, Grant Development and Administration Division, *Report on Fiscal Year 2006 Assistance to Firefighters Grants*, p. 11.

[22] The fire grant program sets a limit of up to three applications per fire department per year (a vehicle application, an application for operations and safety, and a regional application).

Thus, the number of fire departments in a state plays a major factor in the number of fire grant applications submitted and the amount of total funding awarded within a given state. For example, because Pennsylvania has—by far—the largest number of fire departments, it is not surprising that it leads the nation in the number of fire grants applications and the amount of funding awarded.

In: Federal Firefighter Funding and Fire Assistance   ISBN 978-1-62081-176-4
Editors: M. L. Hill and C. F. Green   ©2012 Nova Science Publishers, Inc.

Chapter 2

STAFFING FOR ADEQUATE FIRE AND EMERGENCY RESPONSE: THE SAFER GRANT PROGRAM[*]

Lennard G. Kruger

SUMMARY

In response to concerns over the adequacy of firefighter staffing, the Staffing for Adequate Fire and Emergency Response Act—popularly called the "SAFER Act"—was enacted by the 108th Congress as Section 1057 of the FY2004 National Defense Authorization Act (P.L. 108-136). The SAFER Act authorizes grants to career, volunteer, and combination local fire departments for the purpose of increasing the number of firefighters to help communities meet industry-minimum standards and attain 24-hour staffing to provide adequate protection from fire and fire-related hazards. Also authorized are grants to volunteer fire departments for recruitment and retention of volunteers.

With the economic turndown adversely affecting budgets of local governments, concerns have arisen that modifications to the SAFER statute may be necessary to enable fire departments to more effectively participate in the program. The American Recovery and Reinvestment Act of 2009 (P.L. 111-5) included a provision (§603) that waived the matching requirements for SAFER grants awarded in FY2009 and

---

[*] This is an edited, reformatted and augmented version of Congressional Research Service, Publication No. RL33375., dated January 3, 2012.

FY2010. The FY2009 Supplemental Appropriations Act (P.L. 111- 32) included a provision authorizing the Secretary of Homeland Security to waive further limitations and restrictions in the SAFER statute for FY2009 and FY2010.

The Department of Defense and Continuing Appropriations Act, 2011 (P.L. 112-10) funded SAFER at $405 million. The law also contained language that removes cost-share requirements and allows SAFER grants to be used to rehire laid-off firefighters and fill positions eliminated through attrition. However, P.L. 112-10 did not remove the requirement that SAFER grants fund a firefighter position for four years, with the fifth year funded wholly by the grant recipient. The law also did not waive the cap of $100,000 per firefighter hired by a SAFER grant.

The Administration's FY2012 budget proposed $670 million for firefighter assistance, including $420 million for SAFER, which according to the FY2012 budget proposal, would fund 2,200 firefighter positions. P.L. 112-74, the Consolidated Appropriations Act, FY2012 provided $337.5 million for SAFER, and included language permitting FY2012 grants to be used to rehire laid-off firefighters and fill positions eliminated through attrition, as well as removing other SAFER restrictions and limitations. P.L. 112-74 also reinstated waiver authority for the restrictions that were not lifted in the FY2011 appropriations act (P.L. 112-10).

Concern over local fire departments' budgetary problems has framed debate over the SAFER reauthorization, which is included in S. 550/H.R. 2269, the Fire Grants Authorization Act of 2011. Previously in the 111th Congress, reauthorization legislation for SAFER was passed by the House, but was not passed by the Senate. As part of the reauthorization debate, Congress may consider whether some SAFER rules and restrictions governing the hiring grants should be eliminated or altered in order to make it economically feasible for more fire departments to participate in the program.

BACKGROUND AND GENESIS OF SAFER

Firefighting and the provision of fire protection services to the public is traditionally a local responsibility, funded primarily by state, county, and municipal governments. During the 1990s, however, shortfalls in state and local budgets—coupled with increased responsibilities (i.e., counterterrorism) of local fire departments—led many in the fire community to call for additional financial support from the federal government. Since enactment of the FIRE Act[1] in the 106th Congress, the Assistance to Firefighters Grants (AFG) program (also known as "fire grants" and "FIRE Act grants") has provided funding for equipment and training directly from the federal government to local fire departments.[2]

Since the fire grant program commenced in FY2001, funding has been used by fire departments to purchase firefighting equipment, personal protective equipment, and firefighting vehicles. Many in the fire-service community argued that notwithstanding the fire grant program, there remained a pressing need for an additional federal grant program to assist fire departments in the hiring of firefighters and the recruitment and retention of volunteer firefighters. They asserted that without federal assistance, many local fire departments would continue to be unable to meet national consensus standards for minimum staffing levels, which specify at least four firefighters per responding fire vehicle (or five or six firefighters in hazardous or high-risk areas).[3] Fire-service advocates also pointed to the Community Oriented Policing Services (COPS) program[4] as a compelling precedent of federal assistance for the hiring of local public safety personnel.

In support of SAFER, fire-service advocates cited and continue to cite studies performed by the U.S. Fire Administration and the National Fire Protection Association,[5] the *Boston Globe*,[6] and the National Institute for Occupational Safety and Health (NIOSH)[7] which concluded that many fire departments fall below minimum standards for personnel levels. According to these studies, the result of this shortfall can lead to inadequate response to different types of emergency incidents, substandard response times, and an increased risk of firefighter fatalities.

On the other hand, those opposed to SAFER grants contend that funding for basic local government functions—such as paying for firefighter salaries—should not be assumed by the federal government, particularly at a time of high budget deficits. Also, some SAFER opponents disagree that below-standard levels in firefighting personnel are necessarily problematic, and point to statistics indicating that the number of structural fires in the United States has continued to decline over the past 20 years.[8]

AUTHORIZATION - THE SAFER ACT

In response to concerns over the adequacy of firefighter staffing, the Staffing for Adequate Fire and Emergency Response Act—popularly called the "SAFER Act"—was introduced into the 107th and 108th Congresses.[9] The

**Table 1. Authorization Levels for SAFER Grant Program
(billions of dollars)**

FY2004	FY2005	FY2006	FY2007	FY2008	FY2009	FY2010
1.0	1.03	1.061	1.093	1.126	1.159	1.19

108th Congress enacted the SAFER Act as Section 1057 of the FY2004 National Defense Authorization Act (P.L. 108-136; signed into law November 24, 2003). The SAFER provision was added as an amendment to S. 1050 on the Senate floor (S.Amdt. 785, sponsored by Senator Dodd) and modified in the FY2004 Defense Authorization conference report (H.Rept. 108-354). The SAFER grant program is codified as Section 34 of the Federal Fire Prevention and Control Act of 1974 (15 U.S.C. 2229a).

The SAFER Act authorizes grants to career, volunteer, and combination fire departments for the purpose of increasing the number of firefighters to help communities meet industry-minimum standards and attain 24-hour staffing to provide adequate protection from fire and fire-related hazards. Also authorized are grants to volunteer fire departments for activities related to the recruitment and retention of volunteers. SAFER grants were authorized through FY2010. Table 1 shows the authorization levels for the SAFER grant program.

Two types of grants are authorized by the SAFER Act: hiring grants and recruitment and retention grants. *Hiring grants* cover a four-year term and are cost shared with the local jurisdiction. According to the statute, the federal share shall not exceed 90% in the first year of the grant, 80% in the second year, 50% in the third year, and 30% in the fourth year. The grantee must commit to retaining the firefighter or firefighters hired with the SAFER grant for at least one additional year after the federal money expires. Total federal funding for hiring a firefighter over the four-year grant period may not exceed $100,000, although that total may be adjusted for inflation. While the majority of hiring grants will be awarded to career and combination fire departments, the SAFER Act specifies that 10% of the total SAFER appropriation be awarded to volunteer or majority-volunteer departments for the hiring of personnel.

Additionally, at least 10% of the total SAFER appropriation is set aside for *recruitment and retention grants*, which are available to volunteer and combination fire departments for activities related to the recruitment and retention of volunteer firefighters. Also eligible for recruitment and retention grants are local and statewide organizations that represent the interests of volunteer firefighters. No local cost sharing is required for recruitment and retention grants.

APPROPRIATIONS

The SAFER grant program receives its annual appropriation through the House and Senate Appropriations Subcommittees on Homeland Security. Within the appropriations bills, SAFER is listed under the line item, "Firefighter Assistance Grants," which is located in Title III— Protection, Preparedness, Response, and Recovery. "Firefighter Assistance Grants" also includes the Assistance to Firefighters Grant Program.

Although authorized for FY2004, SAFER did not receive an appropriation in FY2004. Table 2 shows the appropriations history for firefighter assistance, including SAFER, AFG, and the Fire Station Construction Grants (SCG) grants provided in the American Recovery and Reinvestment Act (ARRA). The Bush Administration requested no funding for SAFER in each its budget proposals for FY2005 through FY2009. Table 3 shows recent and proposed appropriated funding for the SAFER and AFG grant programs.

Table 2. Appropriations for Firefighter Assistance, FY2001-FY2012

AFG		SAFER	SCGa	Total
FY2001	$100 million			$100 million
FY2002	$360 million			$360 million
FY2003	$745 million			$745 million
FY2004	$746 million			$746 million
FY2005	$650 million	$65 million		$715 million
FY2006	$539 million	$109 million		$648 million
FY2007	$547 million	$115 million		$662 million
FY2008	$560 million	$190 million		$750 million
FY2009	$565 million	$210 million	$210 million	$985 million
FY2010	$390 million	$420 million		$810 million
FY2011	$405 million	$405 million		$810 million
FY2012	$337.5 million	$337.5 million		$675 million
Total	$5.944 billion	$1.851 billion	$210 million	$8.005 billion

a. Assistance to Firefighters Fire Station Construction Grants (SCG) grants were funded by the American Recovery and Reinvestment Act (P.L. 111-5).

**Table 3. Recent and Proposed Appropriations for Firefighter Assistance
(millions of dollars)**

	FY2010 (Admin. request)	FY2010 (P.L. 111-83)	FY2011 (Admin. request)	FY2011 (P.L. 112-10)	FY2012 (Admin. request)	FY2012 (P.L. 112-74)
FIRE						
Grants						
(AFG)	170	390	305	405	250	337.5
SAFER Grants	420	420	305	405	420	337.5
Total	**590**	**810**	**610**	**810**	**670**	**675**

FY2010

For FY2010, the Obama administration proposed $420 million for SAFER, double the amount appropriated in FY2009. According to the budget justification, this increase will enable fire departments to increase staffing and deployment capabilities to attain 24-hour staffing and ensure that communities have adequate protection from fire and fire-related hazards.

Both the House- and Senate-passed versions of H.R. 2892, the FY2010 Department of Homeland Security appropriations bill, provided $420 million for SAFER in FY2010. According to the House Appropriations Committee (H.Rept. 111-157), the additional funding is part of a targeted and temporary effort to "stem the tide of layoffs and ensure our communities are protected by an adequate number of firefighters." The committee directed FEMA to consider the prospect and occurrence of firefighter layoffs at a local fire department when evaluating SAFER grant applications.

The conference report for the FY2010 Department of Homeland Security Appropriations Act (H.Rept. 111-298) was passed by the House on October 15, 2009, and by the Senate on October 20. H.Rept. 111-298 provided $420 million for SAFER, identical to the levels in both the House and Senate. The bill was signed into law, P.L. 111-83, on October 28, 2009.

FY2011

The Administration's FY2011 budget proposed $305 million for SAFER (a 27% decrease from the FY2010 level) and $305 million for AFG (a 22%

decrease). The total amount requested for firefighter assistance (AFG and SAFER) was $610 million, a 25% decrease from FY2010.

On June 24, 2010, the House Subcommittee on Homeland Security Appropriations approved $840 million for firefighter assistance, including $420 million for SAFER and $420 million for AFG.

On July 19, 2010, the Senate Appropriations Committee approved $810 million for firefighter assistance (including $420 million for SAFER and $390 million for AFG), the same level as FY2010. In the bill report (S.Rept. 111-222), the committee directed DHS to continue funding applications according to local priorities and priorities established by the United States Fire Administration, and to continue direct funding to fire departments and the peer review process.

H.R. 1, the Full-Year Continuing Appropriations Act, 2011, as introduced on February 11, 2011, would have provided zero funding for SAFER and $300 million to AFG. However, on February 16, 2011, H.Amdt. 223 (offered by Representative Pascrell and agreed to by the House by a vote of 318-113) restored SAFER and AFG to FY2010 levels ($420 million and $390 million, respectively). H.R. 1 was passed by the House on February 18, 2011. S.Amdt. 149 to H.R. 1— which was rejected by the full Senate on March 9, 2011— would have funded SAFER at $405 million and AFG at $405 million.

Subsequently, the full-year continuing appropriation bill for FY2011, which was signed into law on April 15, 2011 (Department of Defense and Continuing Appropriations Act, 2011, P.L. 112- 10), funds SAFER at $405 million and AFG at $405 million for FY2011.

FY2012

The Administration's FY2012 budget proposed $670 million for firefighter assistance, including $420 million for SAFER and $250 million for AFG. According to the FY2012 budget proposal, the request would fund 2,200 firefighter positions and approximately 5000 AFG grants.

The Department of Homeland Security Appropriations, 2012, bill (H.R. 2017) was reported by the House Appropriations Committee on May 26, 2011. The House bill, as reported by the committee, would have provided $350 million for firefighter assistance, including $150 million for SAFER and $200 million for AFG. These FY2012 levels would have constituted a 63% cut for SAFER and a 51% cut for AFG compared to the FY2011 appropriation. There was no SAFER waiver language in the committee-approved bill.

The House Appropriations bill report (H.Rept. 112-91) urged DHS to review the costs associated with the SAFER program, noting that "the cost per fighter is extremely high," and that "the budget requests $405 million to enable the hiring of more than 2,200 firefighter positions, or $184,000 per fire-fighter." H.Rept. 112-91 also directed FEMA to continue granting funds directly to local fire departments and to include the United States Fire Administration during the grant decision process.

During the House floor consideration of H.R. 2017, two firefighter assistance amendments were adopted. The first amendment (offered by Representative LaTourette and Representative Pascrell, and agreed to by a recorded vote of 333-87) raised FY2012 funding levels to $335 million for AFG and $335 million for SAFER. The total level for firefighter assistance ($670 million) is equal to the level requested by the Administration.

The second amendment (offered by Representative Price of North Carolina and agreed to by a recorded vote of 264-157) prohibited enforcement of various SAFER requirements for grantees. These waivers would allow FY2012 SAFER grants to be used to rehire laid-off firefighters and fill positions eliminated through attrition, remove cost-share requirements, allow grants to extend longer than the current five year duration, and permit the amount of funding per position at levels exceeding the current limit of $100,000.

The Department of Homeland Security Appropriations, 2012, bill (H.R. 2017) was passed by the House on June 2, 2011.

On September 7, 2011, the Senate Appropriations Committee approved $750 million for firefighter assistance in FY2012 (S.Rept. 112-74), which is a 12% increase over the House-passed level. The total included $375 million for SAFER and $375 million for AFG. As does the House bill, the Senate bill also waived or prohibited SAFER requirements in FY2012. The committee included a provision (§559) which allows SAFER grants to be used to retain firefighters and prohibits or waives SAFER limitations and restrictions. The committee stated its expectation that this provision would be applied in the same manner as similar provisions in the Supplemental Appropriations Act, 2009, and the American Recovery and Reinvestment Act of 2009 for fiscal years 2009 and 2010.

P.L. 112-74, the Consolidated Appropriations Act, FY2012, provided $337.5 million for SAFER, and included language permitting FY2012 grants to be used to rehire laid-off firefighters and fill positions eliminated through attrition, as well as prohibiting DHS from enforcing the other SAFER restrictions and limitations. P.L. 112-74 also reinstated DHS waiver authority for the restrictions that were not lifted in the FY2011 appropriations bill (P.L. 112-10).

SAFER Provisions in Jobs Legislation

The Administration's American Jobs Act (introduced as S. 1549 on September 13, 2011, by Senator Reid, and introduced as H.R. 12 on September 21, 2011, by Representative Larson) would provide $1 billion in additional FY2012 appropriations for SAFER. The legislation would also give DHS the authority to waive SAFER limitations and restrictions. Additionally in the House, H.R. 2914, the Emergency Jobs to Restore the American Dream Act, was introduced by Representative Schakowsky on September 14, 2011. H.R. 2914 would provide $1.2 billion in FY2012 and $1.2 billion in FY2013 for SAFER, and would prohibit the enforcement of SAFER limitations and restrictions. Similar provisions are in the Teachers and First Responders Back to Work Act of 2011 (S. 1723) and the Act for the 99% (H.R. 3638). None of this legislation was passed in the First Session of the 112th Congress.

WAIVER OF SAFER REQUIREMENTS

With the economic turndown adversely affecting budgets of local governments, concerns have arisen that modifications to the SAFER statute may be necessary to enable fire departments to more effectively participate in the program. The American Recovery and Reinvestment Act of 2009 (P.L. 111-5) included a provision (§603) that waived the matching requirements for SAFER grants awarded in FY2009 and FY2010. Currently, according to the statute, the federal share shall not exceed 90% in the first year of the grant, 80% in the second year, 50% in the third year, and 30% in the fourth year.

Subsequently, the FY2009 Supplemental Appropriations Act (P.L. 111-32) included a provision (§605) giving the Secretary of Homeland Security authority to waive certain limitations and restrictions in the SAFER statute. For grants awarded in FY2009 and FY2010, waivers permit grantees to use SAFER funds to rehire laid-off firefighters and fill positions eliminated through attrition, allow grants to extend longer than the current five-year duration, and permit the amount of funding per position at levels exceeding the current limit of $100,000.

Because the SAFER waiver authority in P.L. 111-32 applied only to FY2009 and FY2010, an amendment addressing this issue was offered to H.R. 1, the Full-Year Continuing Appropriations Act, 2011. H.Amdt. 79, offered by Representative Price of North Carolina, stated that none of the funds made available in the FY2011 appropriation may be used to enforce the requirements in the SAFER statute that essentially prohibit using SAFER funds to rehire laid-off firefighters and fill positions eliminated through attrition. Funds would also not be permitted to enforce the five-year duration of the hired position and the limit of $100,000 per hired firefighter. On February 17, 2011, H.Amdt. 79 was agreed to by the House by a vote of 267-159. H.R. 1 was passed by the House on February 18, 2011. S.Amdt. 149 to H.R. 1—which was rejected by the full Senate on March 9, 2011—contains waiver authority which would allow using SAFER funds to rehire laid-off firefighters and fill positions eliminated through attrition. Waivers would also allow exceptions to the requirement for the five-year duration of the hired position and the limit of $100,000 per hired firefighter. Unlike the House-passed version of H.R. 1, the Senate amendment would allow a waiver of cost-share requirements.

The Department of Defense and Continuing Appropriations Act, 2011 (P.L. 112-10) contained language that removes cost-share requirements and allows SAFER grants to be used to rehire laid-off firefighters and fill positions eliminated through attrition. However, the law did not remove the requirement that SAFER grants fund a firefighter position for four years, with the fifth year funded wholly by the grant recipient. P.L. 112-10 also did not waive the cap of $100,000 per firefighter hired by a SAFER grant. According to fire service advocates, these unwaived SAFER requirements (the mandatory five-year position duration, the $100,000 cap) will be a disincentive for many communities to apply for SAFER grants, because localities will be reluctant to apply for grants that would require future expenditure of local funds.[10]

The Department of Homeland Security Appropriations, 2012, bill (H.R. 2017) was passed by the House on June 2, 2011. The House bill, as amended on the House floor, would allow FY2012 grants to be used to rehire laid-off firefighters and fill positions eliminated through attrition, remove cost-share requirements, allow grants to extend longer than the current five year duration, and permit the amount of funding per position at levels exceeding the current limit of $100,000. Similarly, the Senate FY2012 Department of Homeland Security Appropriations bill, as approved by the Senate Appropriations Committee, would maintain waivers and prohibitions of SAFER restrictions as they were applied in FY2009 and FY2010.

Finally, P.L. 112-74, the Consolidated Appropriations Act, FY2012, included language (§561) prohibiting using any funds to enforce all of the SAFER restrictions that have been lifted since FY2009. Additionally, Section 562 of P.L. 112-74 reinstated DHS waiver authority for the restrictions that were not lifted in the FY2011 appropriations bill (P.L. 112-10).

REAUTHORIZATION OF SAFER

The most recent authorization of SAFER expired on September 30, 2010. Previously in the 111th Congress, reauthorization legislation for SAFER and AFG was passed by the House, but was not passed by the Senate. In the 112th Congress, virtually identical versions of the House and Senate bills from the 111th Congress have been introduced.

House Reauthorization of SAFER

On July 8, 2009 (in the 111th Congress), the House Committee on Science and Technology, Subcommittee on Technology and Innovation, held a hearing on the reauthorization of both SAFER and AFG.[11] Testimony was heard from FEMA and many of the major fire-service organizations including the International Association of Fire Chiefs (IAFC), the International Association of Fire Fighters (IAFF), the National Volunteer Fire Council (NVFC), and the National Fire Protection Association (NFPA).

Witnesses asserted that under current economic conditions, many jurisdictions find it difficult to comply with current SAFER statutory restrictions governing the hiring grants sought by career and combination departments. For example, according to the IAFF, DHS data show that "since SAFER's inception four years ago, seventy-eight grantees have had to repay the federal government a total of $62.7 million because they failed to meet the rigorous requirements," and that an "additional seventy-one grants totaling $51.4 million were declined by municipalities that felt they could not meet the program's obligations."[12] According to the IAFC, in 2008, "the DHS reported a greater than 12 percent drop in SAFER grant applications from 2007, including a 20 percent drop in applications from all-career and combination departments with a majority of career firefighters."[13]

According to hearing witnesses, current restrictions that make it difficult for fire departments to use SAFER hiring grants include the requirement that a

SAFER hiring grant extend for five years with an increasing local match required each year (with the fifth year completely funded by the local fire department); the requirement that departments must maintain staffing levels over that five-year period; the statutory cap of $100,000 per firefighter; and restrictions on using SAFER funds to rehire laid-off firefighters and fill positions eliminated through attrition.

The ARRA and the FY2009 Supplemental Appropriations Act gave DHS the authority to waive some of those SAFER restrictions only for FY2009 and FY2010. With respect to the longer-term reauthorization provisions affecting SAFER hiring grants, witnesses at the July 8 hearing recommended

- establishing an across-the-board 20% match rather than the sliding scale under current law;
- shortening the length of the grant period from five years to three years;
- eliminating the funding cap of $100,000 per firefighter for hiring grants that currently cover salary and benefits over a four-year period; and
- making the temporary waiver authority granted in the ARRA and the 2009 Supplemental Appropriations Act permanent, thereby granting DHS authority to waive the restriction on using grants to avoid or reverse layoffs, to waive the local match, and to waive the requirement that personnel levels must be maintained during the life of the grant.

Meanwhile, the NVFC expressed strong support for the recruitment and retention SAFER grants, and argued that in addition to currently eligible state and local interest organizations, national interest organizations should also be eligible for those grants.

On October 13, 2009, H.R. 3791, the Fire Grants Reauthorization Act of 2009, was introduced by Representative Mitchell. The legislation reflected an agreement reached among the major fire service organizations on the reauthorization language. H.R. 3791 was referred to the House Committee on Science and Technology, and approved (amended) by the Subcommittee on Technology and Innovation on October 14, 2009, and by the full committee on October 21, 2009. H.R. 3791 was reported (amended) by the committee on November 7, 2009 (H.Rept. 111-333, Part I), and passed by the House on November 18, 2009.

H.R. 3791, as passed by the House, would have reauthorized SAFER grants at a level of $1.194 billion per year through FY2014. The legislation would modify the SAFER grant program by shortening the grant period to three years, establishing a 20% local matching requirement for each year, removing the existing federal funding cap per hired firefighter, making national organizations eligible for recruitment and retention funds, and allowing DHS in the case of economic hardship to waive cost share requirements, the three-year grant period, and/or maintenance of expenditure requirements.

On June 22, 2011, H.R. 2269, the Fire Grants Reauthorization Act of 2011 was introduced into the 112th Congress by Representative Eddie Bernice Johnson of Texas. H.R. 2269 is virtually identical to H.R. 3791 of the 111th Congress.

Senate Reauthorization of SAFER

On March 10, 2011, S. 550, the Fire Grants Authorization Act of 2011, was introduced by Senator Lieberman, chairman of the Senate Committee on Homeland Security and Governmental Affairs. On May 18, 2011, the Senate Committee on Homeland Security and Governmental Affairs ordered S. 550 to be reported with two amendments. One approved amendment is a requirement that the inspector general of DHS submit to Congress a report detailing whether and to what degree the grant programs are duplicative. The other adopted amendment would sunset both SAFER and AFG grant programs on October 1, 2016, requiring the programs to subsequently be reauthorized past that date in order to continue.

Regarding SAFER, S. 550 would:

- shorten the grant period to three years, with grantees required to retain for at least one year beyond the termination of their grants those firefighters hired under the grant;
- establish a 25% local matching requirement for each year;
- limit the amount of funding provided for hiring a firefighter in any fiscal year at not to exceed 75% of the usual annual cost of a first-year firefighter in that department;
- make national organizations eligible for recruitment and retention funds;

- allow DHS in the case of economic hardship to waive cost share requirements, the required retention period, the prohibition on supplanting local funds, and/or maintenance of expenditure requirements; and
- reauthorize the SAFER grant program from FY2012 through FY2016 at a level of $950 million per year, with each year adjusted for inflation.

In comparison with H.R. 2269, S. 550 has a higher match requirement for hiring grants, retains a maximum amount limit for hiring grants per firefighter, and continues to require applicants to retain hired firefighters for at least one year after the grant expires (unless a waiver is obtained).

IMPLEMENTATION OF THE SAFER PROGRAM

Prior to FY2007, the SAFER grant program was administered by the Office of Grants and Training within the Preparedness Directorate of the Department of Homeland Security (DHS). However, Title VI of the Conference Agreement on the DHS appropriations bill (P.L. 109-295; H.Rept. 109-699), the Post Katrina Emergency Management Reform Act of 2006, transferred most of the existing Preparedness Directorate (including SAFER and fire grants) back to an enhanced FEMA.

Table 4. State-by-State Distribution of SAFER Grants, FY2005-FY2010 (millions of dollars)

	FY2005	FY2006	FY2007	FY2008	FY2009	FY2010	Total
Alabama	1.611	6.215	4.236	7.314	4.288	8.531	32.195
Alaska	1.051	0.205	0.418	1.438	0.328	6.072	9.512
Arizona	1.560	3.559	4.428	6.613	6.768	10.357	33.285
Arkansas	0.394	1.820	0.377	3.834	0.976	2.206	9.607
California	5.221	5.212	4.259	4 .212	31.501	63.13	113.535
Colorado	1.584	3.479	1.730	2.02	0.955	3.384	13.152
Connecticut	0.130	0.191	0.856	3.92	2.214	3.496	10..807
Delaware	0	0.135	0	0.398	0	1.723	2.256
District of Columbia	0	0	0	0	0	0	0
Florida	6.576	9.329	6.217	17.185	24.105	17.721	81.133
Georgia	5.354	2.085	2.842	17.438	4.844	10.384	42.947
Hawaii	0	0	0	1.626	0	0.1	1.726
Idaho	0.063	0.621	0.626	0.774	1.336	2.897	6.317
Illinois	1.340	4.463	9.933	5.85	2.496	10.848	34.93

	FY2005	FY2006	FY2007	FY2008	FY2009	FY2010	Total
Indiana	0	0.099	2.687	4.577	8.295	9.931	25.589
Iowa	0.169	0.144	0.980	1.288	1.045	0.081	3.707
Kansas	0.667	0.045	1.029	1.872	2.806	2.285	8.704
Kentucky	0.152	2.890	0.429	2.466	0.338	0.893	7.168
Louisiana	3.430	3.078	4.728	8.62	10.515	0.182	30.553
Maine	0.081	0	0.316	0.951	0.739	1.047	3.134
Maryland	0.096	1.862	1.526	3.171	4.429	2.145	13.229
Massachusetts	1.300	2.079	4.372	2.690	18.385	34.422	63.248
Michigan	1.759	0.592	0	0.628	13.286	22.493	38.758
Minnesota	0.300	1.089	0.375	3.246	1.256	0.789	7.055
Mississippi	0.756	0.594	0.115	1.608	0	1.209	4.282
Missouri	1.467	3.547	4.551	2.381	1.474	5.618	19.038
Montana	0.034	0.255	2.635	2.955	0.458	0.973	7.31
Nebraska	0	0.873	0.632	1.951	0.802	0.493	4.751
Nevada	1.500	1.714	0.632	0.086	0.577	2.459	6.968
New Hampshire	0.400	1.035	1.528	0.225	0	0.353	3.541
New Jersey	6.374	3.971	2.953	4.389	0.556	56.648	74.891
New Mexico	0	3.123	1.309	0.108	0.499	1.854	6.893
New York	1.540	2.991	2.845	4.412	8.227	18.239	38.254
North Carolina	2.155	5.533	5.371	18.183	2.256	6.375	39.873
North Dakota	0	0.609	0	1.518	1.517	2.139	5.783
Ohio	1.319	1.881	2.255	3.737	29.606	21.04	59.838
Oklahoma	0.147	0.699	0.531	2.782	0	9.127	13.286
Oregon	1.710	2.141	2.649	2.071	0.677	6.814	16.062
Pennsylvania	1.244	1.475	2.633	3.515	1.176	7.926	17.969
Rhode Island	0.400	0	0.105	0	1.561	4.249	6.315
South Carolina	0.456	0.863	3.218	8.158	2.41	2.064	17.169
South Dakota	0.063	0.311	0.211	0.552	0	0.648	1.785
Tennessee	2.700	2.719	3.683	1.856	1.148	7.374	19.48
Texas	0.951	10.961	8.779	19.06	3.158	12.65	55.559
Utah	0.900	3.312	2.098	3.955	1.824	4.583	16.672
Vermont	0	0.621	0.632	0	0.119	0	1.372
Virginia	2.091	3.554	0.782	1.849	4.891	8.995	22.162
Washington	2.298	2.897	7.340	9.476	2.847	13.779	38.637
West Virginia	0	0.187	0.681	0.16	0.287	0.398	1.713
Wisconsin	0	0.072	1.223	4.502	0	0.12	5.917
Wyoming	0	0	0.316	2.329	0.263	0.997	3.905
Puerto Rico	0	0	0	0	0	0	0
Northern Mariana Islands	0	0	0	0	0	1.404	1.404
Marshall Islands	0	0	0	0	0	0	0
Guam	0	0	0	0	0	0	0
American Samoa	0	0	0	0	0	0	0
Virgin Islands	0	0	0	0	0	0	0
Republic of Palau	0	0	0	0	0	0	0
Total	**61.356**	**105.142**	**113.665**	**203.964**	**207.258**	**413.017**	**1104.402**

Source: Department of Homeland Security. Current as of October 7, 2011.

Table 4 shows the state-by-state distribution of SAFER grant funds, from FY2005 through FY2010. Of the total federal share requested for FY2009, 54.6% was requested by all paid/career departments, 9.3% by all volunteer, 14.7% by combination (majority paid/career), and 19% by combination (majority volunteer).[14] Of the FY2010 SAFER awards, grants for hiring accounted for 84.3% of the total federal share awarded. For the latest information and updates on the application for and awarding of SAFER grants, see the official SAFER grant program website at http://www.fema.gov /firegrants/safer/index.shtm.

End Notes

[1] Title XVII of the FY2001 Floyd D. Spence National Defense Authorization Act (P.L. 106-398).

[2] For more information, see CRS Report RL32341, *Assistance to Firefighters Program: Distribution of Fire Grant Funding*, by Lennard G. Kruger.

[3] These refer to consensus standards developed by the National Fire Protection Association (NFPA): NFPA 1710 ("Standard for the Organization and Deployment of Fire Suppression Operations, Emergency Medical Operations, and Special Operations to the Public by Career Fire Departments"), and NFPA 1720 ("Standard for the Organization and Deployment of Fire Suppression Operations, Emergency Medical Operations, and Special Operations to the Public by Volunteer Fire Departments"). NFPA standards are voluntary unless adopted as law by governments at the local, state, or federal level, and are also often considered by insurance companies when establishing rates. Another applicable standard to this debate is the federal Occupational Safety and Health Administration (OSHA) standard on respiratory protection in structural firefighting situations (29 CFR 1910.134(g)), which requires at least four firefighters (two in and two for backup) before entering a hazardous environment wearing a Self-Contained Breathing Apparatus.

[4] For more information on the COPS program, see CRS Report RL33308, *Community Oriented Policing Services (COPS): Background and Funding*, by Nathan James.

[5] National Fire Protection Association, *Third Needs Assessment of the U.S. Fire Service*, June 2011, available at http://www.nfpa.org/assets/files//2011NeedsAssessment.pdf.

[6] Dedman, Bill, "Deadly Delays: The Decline of Fire Response," *Boston Globe Special Report*, January 30, 2005. Available at http://www.boston.com/news/specials/fires/.

[7] National Institute for Occupational Safety and Health, "National Institute for Occupational Safety and Health (NIOSH) Fire Fighter Fatality Investigation and Prevention Program, 1998 - 2005," March 2006, 16 p. Available at http://www.cdc.gov/niosh/fire/pdfs /progress.pdf.

[8] See Lehrer, Eli, "Do We Need More Firefighters?" *Weekly Standard,* April 12, 2004, p. 21-22. Available at http://www.sipr.org/default.aspx?action=PublicationDetails&id=44. See also Easterbrook, Gregg, "Where's the Fire?" *New Republic Online*, August 9, 2004. Available at http://www.tnr.com/doc.mhtml?i=express&s=easterbrook080904.

[9] 107th Congress: S. 1617 (Dodd), H.R. 3992 (Boehlert), H.R. 3185 (Green, Gene). 108th Congress: S. 544 (Dodd), H.R. 1118 (Boehlert).

[10] International Association of Fire Fighters, *News Release*, "Budget: Agreement Retains Level Funding for FIRE Act and SAFER grants, But Restricts Flexibility on SAFER Grants," April 14, 2011, available at http://www.iaff.org/ 11News/041311Waivers.htm.

[11] See http://science.house.gov/publications/hearings_markups_details.aspx?NewsID=2539.

[12] Kevin O'Connor, Assistant to the General President, International Association of Fire Fighters, written statement before the House Subcommittee on Technology and Innovation, Committee on Science and Technology, July 8, 2009, p. 8,
http://democrats.science.house.gov/Media/file/Commdocs/hearings/2009/Tech/8jul/O'Connor_Testimony.pdf.

[13] Jeffrey Johnson, First Vice President, International Association of Fire Chiefs, written statement before the House Subcommittee on Technology and Innovation, Committee on Science and Technology, July 8, 2009, p. 6, http://democrats.science.house.gov/Media/file/Commdocs/hearings/2009/Tech/8jul/Johnson_Testimony.pdf.

[14] Latest SAFER application statistics are available at http://www.fema.gov/firegrants/safer/statistics.shtm.

In: Federal Firefighter Funding and Fire Assistance   ISBN 978-1-62081-176-4
Editors: M. L. Hill and C. F. Green   ©2012 Nova Science Publishers, Inc.

Chapter 3

FEDERAL FUNDING FOR WILDFIRE CONTROL AND MANAGEMENT[*]

Ross W. Gorte

SUMMARY

The Forest Service (FS) and the Department of the Interior (DOI) are responsible for protecting most federal lands from wildfires. Wildfire appropriations nearly doubled in FY2001, following a severe fire season in the summer of 2000, and have remained at relatively high levels. The acres burned annually have also increased over the past 50 years, with the six highest annual totals occurring since 2000. Many in Congress are concerned that wildfire costs are spiraling upward without a reduction in damages. With emergency supplemental funding, FY2008 wildfire funding was $4.46 billion, more than in any previous year.

The vast majority (about 95%) of federal wildfire funds are spent to protect federal lands—for fire preparedness (equipment, baseline personnel, and training); fire suppression operations (including emergency funding); post-fire rehabilitation (to help sites recover after the wildfire); and fuel reduction (to reduce wildfire damages by reducing fuel levels). Since FY2001, FS fire appropriations have included funds for state fire assistance, volunteer fire assistance, and forest health management (to supplement other funds for these three programs),

---

[*] This is an edited, reformatted and augmented version of Congressional Research Service, Publication No. RL33990, dated July 5, 2011.

economic action and community assistance, fire research, and fire facilities.

Four issues have dominated wildfire funding debates. One is the high cost of fire management and its effects on other agency programs. Several studies have recommended actions to try to control wildfire costs, and the agencies have taken various steps, but it is unclear whether these actions will be sufficient. Borrowing to pay high wildfire suppression costs has affected other agency programs. The Federal Land Assistance, Management, and Enhancement (FLAME) Act was enacted in P.L. 111-88 to insulate other agency programs from high wildfire suppression costs by creating a separate funding structure for emergency supplemental wildfire suppression efforts.

Another issue is funding for fuel reduction. Funding and acres treated rose (roughly doubling) between FY2000 and FY2003, and have stabilized since. Currently about 3 million acres are treated annually. However, 75 million acres of federal land are at high risk, and another 156 million acres are at moderate risk, of ecological damage from catastrophic wildfire. Since many ecosystems need to be treated on a 10-35 year cycle (depending on the ecosystem), current treatment rates are insufficient to address the problem.

A third issue is the federal role in protecting nonfederal lands, communities, and private structures. In 1994, federal firefighting resources were apparently used to protect private residences at a cost to federal lands and resources in one severe fire. A federal policy review recommended increased state and local efforts to match their responsibilities, but federal programs to protect nonfederal lands have also expanded, reducing incentives for local participation in fire protection.

Finally, post-fire rehabilitation is raising concerns. Agency regulations and legislation in the 109th Congress focused on expediting such activities, but opponents expressed concerns that this would restrict environmental review of and public involvement in salvage logging decisions, leading to greater environmental damage. Legislation was introduced but not enacted in the 110th Congress to provide alternative means of addressing post-fire restoration in particular areas. The large wildfires to date in 2011 have reignited concerns about post-fire rehabilitation.

Severe fire seasons in the past decade have prompted substantial debate and proposals related to fire protection programs and funding. President Clinton proposed a new National Fire Plan in 2000 to increase funding to protect federal, state, and private lands; Congress largely enacted this request. The severe 2002 fire season led President Bush to propose a Healthy Forests Initiative to expedite fuel reduction on federal lands. In 2003, Congress enacted the Healthy Forests Restoration Act to expedite fuel reduction on federal lands and to authorize other forest protection programs. In 2009, Congress enacted the Federal Land Assistance, Management, and Enhancement (FLAME) Act to insulate other agency programs from high wildfire suppression costs.

Wildfire funding has continued at relatively high levels since 2000, and now constitutes a substantial portion of land management agency budgets. Severe fire seasons seem to have become more common since 2000. (See Figure 1.) Total wildfire funding for FY2008 was a record high of $4.46 billion. The high costs of firefighting continue to attract attention.

Fire Seasons and Fiscal Years

Wildfire data can be confusing because fire seasons and fiscal years rarely match, Fire seasons begin in spring and may run through November. Emergency funding is often enacted after the fire season is nearly complete. Thus, wildfire control funding is commonly high in the fiscal year following a severe fire season. The severe 2000 fire season, for example, led to much higher appropriations for wildfire in FY2001.

This report briefly describes the three categories of federal programs for wildfire protection. One is to protect the federal lands managed by the U.S. Department of Agriculture's Forest Service (FS), and by the U.S. Department of the Interior (DOI), whose wildfire programs traditionally were funded through the Bureau of Land Management (BLM) but are now a department-wide funding item. A second category assists state and local governments and communities in protecting nonfederal lands; these programs can be used by the state and local governments to reduce wildland fuels, to otherwise prepare for fire control, to contain and control wildfires, and to respond after severe wildfires have burned. A third category of federal programs supports fire research, fire facilities, and improvements in forest health. The last section of this report discusses issues associated with the high wildfire costs, including pending legislation.

BACKGROUND

The FS was created in 1905 with the merger of the USDA Bureau of Forestry (which conducted research and provided technical assistance to states and private landowners) and the Forestry Division of the General Land Office (a predecessor of the BLM). An early focus was on halting wildfires in the national forests following several large fires that burned nearly 5 million acres in Montana and Idaho in 1910.[1] Efforts to control wildfires were founded on a belief that fast, aggressive control was efficient, because fires that were stopped while small would not become the large, destructive conflagrations that are so expensive to control. The goals were to protect human lives, then private property, then natural resources. In 1926, the agency developed its *10-acre policy*—that all wildfires should be controlled before they reached 10 acres in size—clearly aimed at keeping wildfires small.[2] Then, in 1935, the FS added its *10:00 a.m. policy*—that, for fires exceeding 10 acres, efforts should focus on control before the next burning period began (at 10:00 a.m.). Under the 10:00 a.m. policy, the goal in suppressing large fires is to gain control during the relatively cool and calm conditions of night and early morning, rather than spending major efforts during the heat of the day.

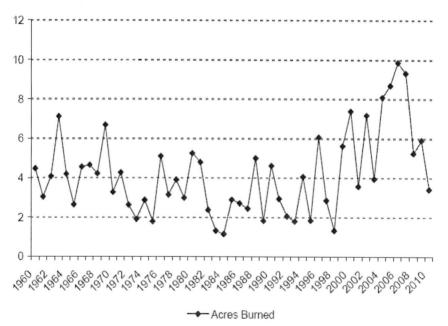

Source: National Interagency Fire Center, at http://www.nifc.gov/fire_info /fires_acres .htm. Note that data for 1983-1991 have been revised downward.
Note: Data are shown in the Appendix.

Figure 1. Acres Burned Annually, (millions of acres).

In the 1970s, these aggressive FS fire control policies began to be questioned. Research had documented that, in some situations, wildfires brought ecological benefits to the burned areas— aiding regeneration of native flora, improving the habitat of native fauna, and reducing infestations of pests and of exotic and invasive species. The Office of Management and Budget challenged as excessive proposed budget increases based on FS policies, and a subsequent study suggested that the fire control policies would increase expenditures beyond efficient levels.[3]

Following the 1988 fires in Yellowstone, concerns were raised about unnaturally high fuel loads leading to catastrophic fires and spiraling suppression costs. Congress established the National Commission on Wildfire Disasters, whose 1994 report described a situation of dangerously high fuel accumulations.[4] The summer of 1994 was another severe fire season, leading to more calls for action to prevent future severe fire seasons. In addition to the concerns about fuel loads, concerns were voiced that, in a fire in Washington in 1994, federal firefighting resources had been diverted from protecting federal lands and resources to protecting nearby private residences and communities.[5] The Clinton administration directed a review of federal fire policy, and the agencies released the new *Federal Wildland Fire Management Policy & Program Review: Final Report* in December 1995. The report recommended altering federal fire policy from priority for private property to equal priority for private property and federal resources, based on values at risk. (Protecting human life is the first priority in firefighting.) The recommended change became effective after the report was accepted by the Secretaries of Agriculture and the Interior.

Concerns about wildfire threats persist. In 1999, the General Accounting Office (GAO, now the Government Accountability Office) issued two reports recommending a cohesive wildfire protection strategy for the FS and a combined strategy for the FS and BLM to address certain firefighting weaknesses.[6] GAO reiterated the need for a cohesive strategy in 2009.[7] To address the severe 2000 fire season, the Clinton administration developed the National Fire Plan and a supplemental budget request. Congress enacted this additional funding in the FY2001 Interior appropriations act, and has since largely maintained the higher funding. (See Figure 2 and Table A-2.) During the severe 2002 fire season, the Bush administration developed the Healthy Forests Initiative to expedite fuel reduction projects in priority areas through administrative and legislative changes. Some elements of the initiative have been addressed through regulatory changes; others were addressed in the Healthy Forests Restoration Act of 2003 (P.L. 108-148).

FUNDING LEVELS

Wildfire management appropriations have risen over the past 15 years, as shown in Figure 2. The tables below present data on funding for the three categories of federal fire programs—protection of federal lands (Table 1 and Table 2); assistance for protection of nonfederal lands (Table 3 and Table 4); and other fire-related expenditures (also Table 3 and Table 4). The FS and DOI use three fire appropriation accounts—preparedness, suppression operations, and other operations— to fund most federal fire programs. However, the agencies include different activities in the accounts (e.g., the BLM historically included fire research and fire facility funding in the preparedness account), and the accounts change over time (e.g., the agencies split operations funding into suppression and other operations in 2001). Thus, the data, taken from the agency budget justifications for the National Fire Plan, have been rearranged in this report to present consistent data and trends on the three categories of federal wildfire programs since 1999.

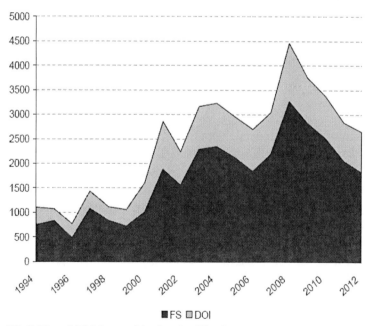

Source: FS, DOI, and BLM annual budget justifications.
Note: Data are shown in the Appendix. Data are not adjusted for inflation.

Figure 2.Wildland Fire Management Appropriations, 1994-2011, (millions of dollars).

Table 1. Historic Wildfire Funding to Protect Federal Lands, FY1999-FY2007
($ in millions)

	FY1999	FY2000	FY2001	FY2002	FY2003	FY2004	FY2005	FY2006	FY2007
Forest Service	**722.4**	**1,008.0**	**1,702.4**	**1,415.6**	**2,162.7**	**2,233.2**	**2,026.2**	**1,737.2**	**2,074.3**
Preparedness	374.8	408.8	611.1	622.6	612.0	671.6	676.5	660.7	655.4
Suppression	180.6	139.2	319.3	255.3	418.0	597.1	648.9	690.2	741.5
Emergency Funds a	102.0	390.0	425.1	266.0	889.0	699.2	395.5	100.0	370.0
Site Rehabilitation	0.0	0.0	141.7	62.7	7.1	6.9	12.8	6.2	6.2
Fuel Reduction	65.0	70.0	205.2	209.0	236.6	258.3	292.5	280.1	301.3
DOI	**327.9**	**577.7**	**929.1**	**640.6**	**845.0**	**853.6**	**801.3**	**831.8**	**841.6**
Preparedness b	147.9	152.6	276.7	253.0	255.2	254.2	258.9	268.8	274.8
Suppression	96.2	158.1	153.1	127.4	159.3	192.9	218.4	230.7	249.2
Emergency Funds a	50.0	200.0	199.6	54.0	225.0	198.4	98.6	100.0	95.0
Site Rehabilitation	0.0c	20.0	104.8	20.0	19.9	24.2	23.9	24.1	22.8
Fuel Reduction	33.8d	47.0	195.0	186.2	185.6	183.9	201.4	208.1	199.8
Total	**1,050.3**	**1,585.6**	**2,631.5**	**2,056.3**	**3,007.6**	**3,086.8**	**2,827.5**	**2,569.0**	**2,915.9**
Preparedness	522.7	561.3	887.9	875.7	867.2	925.8	935.4	929.5	930.2
Suppression	276.8	297.3	472.4	382.7	577.3	790.0	867.3	920.9	990.7
Emergency Funds a	152.0	590.0	624.6	320.0	1,114.0	897.6	494.1	200.0	465.0
Site Rehabilitation	0.0	20.0	246.6	82.7	26.9	31.1	36.8	30.3	29.0
Fuel Reduction	98.8	117.0	400.1	395.2	422.3	442.2	493.9	488.2	501.0

Source: Annual agency budget justifications.

a Excludes emergency funds provided for other specified activities, such as site rehabilitation, fuel reduction, or state assistance.

b Excludes joint fire science research and facilities funding enacted within the BLM preparedness account through FY2004

c Unidentified amount included in suppression funding.

d Calculated at 26% of wildfire operations (see page IV-36 of the FY2001 BLM budget justification).

Federal Lands

Many wildfire management funds are used to protect federal lands. Table 1 shows wildfire management appropriations for FY1999-FY2007; more recent data are shown in Table 2. The data in these tables exclude funding for the other two categories of federal wildfire funding— assistance to state and local governments, communities, and private landowners; and other fire-related activities (research, fire facility maintenance, forest health improvement, etc.). The BLM included funds for fire research and fire facilities under its preparedness budget line item through FY2004; these funds have been excluded from Table 1. The tables show appropriations by fiscal year, with emergency funding identified for the year in which it was provided, rather than in the year it was spent. The agencies traditionally were authorized to borrow from other accounts for fire suppression, and emergency funds generally repay these borrowings. The tables show that total federal land fire management appropriations rose substantially in FY2001 and have since remained relatively high, with fluctuations generally depending on the severity of the fire season in the preceding calendar year.

Preparedness

Fire preparedness appropriations provide funding for fire prevention and detection as well as for equipment, training, and baseline personnel. Preparedness funding rose substantially (58%) in FY2001 from the prior year, with DOI funding rising more (81%) than FS funding (49%). In FY2004, preparedness funding rose by a lesser amount (7%), with the rise entirely in FS preparedness. (DOI preparedness funding declined slightly.) Funding was relatively stable for FY2004 through FY2011. However, for FY2012, the budget request proposed a substantial ($332 million, 49%) increase in FS preparedness, and a modest ($14 million, 5%) decline in DOI preparedness. The budget overview notes that the increase in FS preparedness (and roughly comparable decline in suppression funding) stems from a realignment of various preparedness costs that were shifted to the suppression account over the previous several fiscal years.

Suppression and Emergency Funds

Funds for fighting wildfires—appropriations for fire suppression and supplemental, contingency, or emergency funds—have fluctuated widely over the past decade, from less than $430 million in FY1999 to $2.41 billion in FY2008.

**Table 2. Recent Wildfire Funding to Protect Federal Lands,
FY2008-Present, ($ in millions)**

	FY2008 Actual	FY2009 Totala	FY2010 Actualb	FY2011 Enactedc	FY2012 Requestd
Forest Service	**3,003.4**	**2,453.5**	**2,367.4**	**1,916.7**	**1,725.7**
Preparedness	690.8	675.0	675.0	673.7	1,006.1
Suppression	845.6	993.9	997.5	995.5	538.7
*Emergency Funds*e	932.0	200.0	413.0	90.4	315.9
Site Rehabilitation	110.8	11.5	11.6	11.5	0.0
*Fuel Reduction*f	410.1	584.6	345.3	344.6	57.0g
DOI	**1,174.1**	**905.3**	**836.8**	**766.8**	**809.4**
Preparedness	276.5	281.8	290.5	290.5	277.0
Suppression	289.8	335.2	383.8	399.0	270.6
*Emergency Funds*e	343.0	50.0	61.0	60.9	92.0
Site Rehabilitation	55.2	20.3	20.3	33.2	13.0
Fuel Reduction	209.6	218.1	206.2	183.3	156.8
Total	**4,177.5**	**3,358.8**	**3,442.6**	**2,682.4**	**2,535.1**
Preparedness	967.3	956.8	965.5	964.1	1,283.0
Suppression	1,135.4	1,329.1	1,381.3	1,394.5	809.3
*Emergency Funds*e	1,275.0	250.0	494.0	151.3	407.9
Site Rehabilitation	166.0	31.8	31.9	44.7	13.0
Fuel Reduction	619.7	791.1	551.5	527.9	213.8

Source: Annual agency budget justifications and conference agreements on P.L. 110-116, P.L. 110-161, P.L. 110-329, P.L. 111-5, P.L. 111-8, P.L. 111-88, and data from the House Appropriations Subcommittee on Interior, Environment, and Related Agencies.

a Includes funding in P.L. 111-8 and P.L. 111-32 as well as in P.L. 111-5, the American Recovery and Reinvestment Act of 2009 (ARRA). ARRA funds were available for use in FY2009 or FY2010.

b Totals reflect savings of $75.0 million from FS use of prior-year funds and $125.0 million from BLM use of prior-year funds.

c Reflects across-the-board 0.2% reduction as well as rescissions of $200.0 million from FS wildland fire management appropriations, $200.0 million from FS FLAME fund appropriations, and $200.0 million from DOI wildland fire management appropriations.

d Reflects a rescission of $192 million from FS wildland fire management appropriations.

e Since FY2010, reflects appropriations to (and rescissions from) the FLAME funds. Excludes emergency funds provided for other specified activities, such as site rehabilitation, fuel reduction, or state assistance.

f Excludes funds used for biomass grants ($5.0 million annually, FY2009-FY2012), Community Wood Energy Program ($5.0 million in FY2011), and Forest Biomass for Energy Program ($15.0 million in FY2011). These funds could be used for energy from federal land biomass, but could also be used for energy from nonfederal land biomass. Thus, the funds are listed below under assistance programs.

g Reflects data reported by the House Appropriations Subcommittee on Interior, Environment, and Related Agencies; the FS FY2012 budget justification shows $254.0 million and notes that fuel reduction on lands not in the Wildland-Urban Interface will be funded from a new National Forest System line item for Integrated Resource Restoration.

Some of the variation results from differences in the severity of the fire season in the preceding year, particularly for supplemental and emergency funding. Such fluctuations have long been part of the agencies' funding; for example, total appropriations in FY1997 were double the FY1996 levels owing to a severe season in the summer of 1996. Appropriations for fire suppression rose steadily and sharply for both agencies from FY2002 through FY2008, then stabilized through FY2011. The FY2012 budget request proposed substantial reduction in suppression appropriations—down $457 million (46%) for FS fire suppression and $128 million (32%) for DOI fire suppression. However, this was offset by proposed increases in supplemental, contingency, and emergency funds.

Title V of the FY2010 Interior, Environment, and Related Agencies Appropriations Act (P.L. 111- 88) was the Federal Land Assistance, Management, and Enhancement (FLAME) Act. This title established FLAME Wildfire Suppression Reserve Accounts for the FS and DOI, to be funded from annual appropriations. The FLAME funds can be used if the Secretary declares that (1) an individual wildfire covers at least 300 acres or threatens lives, property, or resources, or (2) cumulative wildfire suppression and emergency response costs will exceed, within 30 days, appropriations for wildfire suppression and emergency responses. The FY2010 act also included $413 million for the FS FLAME fund and $61 million for the DOI FLAME fund. For FY2011, FLAME fund appropriations were much lower for the FS—$90 million (including the $200 million rescission)—while being stable for DOI. Foy FY2012, the budget request included $316 million for the FS FLAME fund and $92 million for the DOI FLAME fund.

The sum total of these accounts for wildfire suppression for FY2012 was less than the total funds available for wildfire suppression in FY2010 or FY2011. For the FS, the request totaled $855 million ($539 million in the suppression account, $316 million in the FLAME fund); this is $231 million (21%) less than the FY2011 funding total of $1.09 billion, and $556 million (39%) less than the FY2010 funding total of $1.41 billion. For DOI, the request totaled $363 million ($271 million in the suppression account, $92 million in the FLAME fund); this is $97 million (21%) less than the FY2011 funding total of $460 million, and $82 million (18%) less than the FY2010 funding total of $445 million.

Post-Fire Rehabilitation

Wildfire appropriations for rehabilitating burned areas have been relatively stable, except in a few fiscal years. Most wildfire site rehabilitation funds have been to the BLM for treating burned DOI lands. Except for a fivefold increase for FY2001 and a doubling in FY2008, DOI site rehabilitation funds generally have ranged between $20 and $25 million annually since FY2000. For FY2012, proposed DOI site rehabilitation funding was $13 million, down $20 million (61%) from FY2011.

The FS generally receives few wildfire funds for site rehabilitation (none prior to FY2001), and instead uses funds appropriated to other accounts, such as watershed improvement and vegetation management. However, the FS was appropriated $142 million of wildfire funds for site rehabilitation in FY2001, $63 million in FY2002, and $111 million in FY2008 (including $100 million in emergency supplemental funding). These three years account for 81% of FS wildfire appropriations for site rehabilitation since FY2000. For FY2012, no funding was proposed for FS site rehabilitation.

Fuel Reduction[8]

Fuel reduction funding is intended to protect lands and resources from wildfire damages by lowering the fuel loads on federal lands, and thus making the fires less intense and more controllable. Total fuel reduction funding more than tripled in FY2001. Fuel reduction funding rose slowly from FY2001 through FY2007. Funding rose substantially (24%) in FY2008 and again in FY2009 (another 28%), owing to funding in the economic stimulus, P.L. 111-5 (the American Recovery and Reinvestment Act of 2009). For FY2010, the appropriations declined substantially (41% for the FS and 5% for DOI), and FY2011 appropriations were lower still (down slightly for the FS and down another 11% for DOI).

Further declines were proposed for FY2012. Proposed DOI fuel reduction funding for FY2012 was $157 million, 14% below FY2011, which was the lowest level since FY2000. For the FS, the fuel reduction funding request for FY2012 is harder to discern, because the FS proposed shifting fuel reduction funding for areas outside the Wildland-Urban Interface (WUI) into a new line item within the National Forest System account—Integrated Resource Restoration—along with funding from several other line items. Within the FS Wildland Fire Management account, fuel reduction was proposed to decline to $57 million.[9]

Some FS fuel reduction funds have been used and proposed for wood energy programs. For FY2009-FY2012, $5 million annually was used for biomass grants. In FY2010, $10.0 million was used for the Collaborative Forest Landscape Restoration Fund, to be used in large part to restore national forest landscapes through fuel reduction, and thus is included in the fuel reduction funding in Table 1. (In FY2011, this program was funded within the National Forest System account, and was proposed to be included in the new Integrated Resource Restoration line item for FY2012.) These programs can contribute to fuel reduction for the national forests, since they provide markets for the fuels to be removed. However, they are not limited to woody biomass from national forests, and no allocation of funding between fuels from national forests and biomass from nonfederal lands is specified. Thus, these programs are included below, under assistance for nonfederal lands.

Assistance for Nonfederal Lands

States are responsible for fire protection of nonfederal lands, except for lands protected by the federal agencies under cooperative agreements. The federal government, primarily through the FS, has a group of wildfire programs to provide assistance to states, local governments, and communities to protect nonfederal (both government and private) lands from wildfire damages.

Most FS fire assistance programs are funded under the agency's State and Private Forestry (S&PF) branch.[10] State fire assistance includes financial and technical help for fire prevention, fire control, and prescribed fire use for state foresters, and through them, for other agencies and organizations. In cooperation with the General Services Administration (GSA), the FS is encouraged to transfer "excess personal property" (equipment) from federal agencies to state and local firefighting forces. The FS also provides assistance directly to volunteer fire departments. Since FY2001, fire assistance funding also has come through wildfire appropriations. The economic stimulus legislation, P.L. 111-5, contained wildfire funds for state and private forestry activities, including fuel reduction, forest health improvement activities (discussed under "Other Fire Funding," below), and wood energy grants. In addition, the 2002 farm bill (P.L. 107-171) created a new community fire protection program, authorizing the FS to assist communities in protecting themselves from wildfires and to act on nonfederal lands (with the consent of landowners) to assist in protecting structures and communities from wildfires. The 2008 farm bill (P.L. 110-246) created two biomass energy grant programs—the Community Wood Energy Program and the Forest Biomass for Energy Program. These subsidies may stimulate markets for fuel removed from nonfederal lands for wildfire protection.

Wildfire funds have also been provided for economic assistance. For three years (FY2001- FY2003), FS wildfire appropriations were added to the S&PF Economic Action Program (EAP) for training and for loans to existing or new ventures to help local economies. In addition, in FY2001, the FS received fire funds to directly aid communities recovering from the severe fires in 2000. DOI also received funding to assist rural areas affected by wildfires for FY2001 through FY2010 (except for FY2007).

Total assistance funds for protecting nonfederal lands increased substantially in FY2001, from $27 million (all FS S&PF funds) to $148 million. Funding dropped about 20% in FY2002 (to $118 million) and fluctuated widely (by as much as 35% annually) through FY2007. Funding nearly tripled in FY2008, and jumped again (up another 42%) in FY2009. In FY2010, funding fell substantially (by 63%), to below the FY2001 level. Funding fell (by another 12%) in FY2011 and was proposed to continue the downward trend in FY2012, falling by another 18%. Funding for assistance programs is shown in Table 3 and Table 4.

Wildfire funds for assistance programs were enacted initially in FY2001, and have been maintained for FS state and volunteer assistance programs. For FY2008, some of the emergency funds provided for FS fuel reduction (in P.L. 110-116 and in P.L. 110-329) were directed to fuel reduction on nonfederal lands; these funds have been included in state fire assistance in Table 4, and excluded from Table 2. FS wildfire funding for state fire assistance more than quadrupled in FY2008, and rose another 50% in FY2009, with funding in the economic stimulus. Funding declined substantially (by 74%) in FY2010, fell further (by 9%) in FY2011, and was proposed to decline again (by 30%) in FY2012.

FS community assistance to aid communities affected by fires in the summer of 2000 was a onetime appropriation, and FS EAP funds from wildfire appropriations were enacted for only three years. Appropriations for DOI rural assistance were provided annually from FY2001 through FY2010, except for FY2007. However, no funds were provided for FY2011 and none were requested for FY2012.

In contrast, funding for FS biomass energy programs has been stable. The initial stimulus was $5 million in annual appropriations and $50 million from P.L. 111-5, the economic stimulus act, in FY2009. Since then, funding has been $5 million annually. The sustained funding reflects interest in fuel reduction, particularly on federal lands for wildfire protection, combined with the desire to produce renewable energy and transportation fuels. While some renewable and bioenergy programs allow biomass fuels from federal lands, others restrict such use.[11]

Table 3. Historic Federal Funding to Assist in Protecting Nonfederal Lands and for Other Purposes, FY1999-FY2007 ($ in millions; includes emergency appropriations)

	FY1999	FY2000	FY2001	FY2002	FY2003	FY2004	FY2005	FY2006	FY2007
FS, Wildfire Mgt.	0.0	0.0	108.5	77.1	79.4	59.2	48.1	53.6	54.0
State Fire Assistance	*0.0*	*0.0*	*52.9*	*56.4*	*66.3*	*51.1*	*40.2*	*45.8*	*46.2*
Volunteer Fire Asst.	*0.0*	*0.0*	*8.3*	*8.3*	*8.2*	*8.1*	*7.9*	*7.8*	*7.8*
Economic Action	*0.0*	*0.0*	*12.5*	*12.5*	*5.0*	*0.0*	*0.0*	*0.0*	*0.0*
Community Asst.	*0.0*	*0.0*	*34.9*	*0.0*	*0.0*	*0.0*	*0.0*	*0.0*	*0.0*
DOI Rural Assistance	0.0	0.0	10.0	10.0	9.9	9.9	9.9	9.9	0.0
Total Wildfire Funds	**0.0**	**0.0**	**118.5**	**87.1**	**89.3**	**69.1**	**58.9**	**63.4**	**54.0**
Forest Service, S&PF	22.9	27.2	29.9	30.4	30.5	63.3	38.8	38.8	38.8
State Fire Assistance	*20.9*	*23.9*	*24.9*	*25.3*	*25.5*	*58.2*	*32.9*	*32.9*	*32.9*
Volunteer Fire Asst.	*2.0*	*3.2*	*5.0*	*5.1*	*5.0*	*5.0*	*5.9*	*5.9*	*5.9*
Total Assistance for Nonfederal Lands	**22.9**	**27.2**	**148.5**	**117.5**	**119.8**	**132.4**	**97.8**	**102.2**	**92.8**
FS, Wildfire Mgt.	0.0	0.0	71.8	67.6	47.9	54.6	54.3	55.3	55.3
Joint Fire Science	*0.0*	*0.0*	*0.0*	*8.0*	*7.9*	*7.9*	*7.9*	*7.9*	*7.9*
Fire research	*0.0*	*0.0*	*16.0*	*27.3*	*21.3*	*22.0*	*21.7*	*22.8*	*22.8*
Fire facilities	*0.0*	*0.0*	*43.9*	*20.4*	*1.8*	*0.0*	*0.0*	*0.0*	*0.0*
Forest health	*0.0*	*0.0*	*12.0*	*12.0*	*16.8*	*24.7*	*24.7*	*24.6*	*24.6*
DOI	9.0	13.3	38.0	27.8	20.2	20.1	20.1	13.6	11.7
Joint Fire Science	*4.0*	*4.0*	*8.0*	*8.0*	*7.9*	*7.9*	*7.9*	*5.9*	*4.0*
Fire facilities	*5.0*	*9.3*	*30.0*	*19.8*	*12.3*	*12.2*	*12.2*	*7.7*	*7.7*
Total Wildfire Funds for Other Purposes	**9.0**	**13.3**	**109.8**	**95.4**	**68.1**	**74.7**	**74.4**	**68.9**	**67.0**

Source: Annual agency budget justifications.

**Table 4. Recent Federal Funding to Assist in Protecting
Nonfederal Lands and for Other Purposes, FY2008-Present
($ in millions)**

	FY2008	FY2009a	FY2010	FY2011 Enactedb	FY2012 Request
FS, Wildfire Mgt.	210.8	314.0	80.3	78.9	56.9
State Fire Assistance	*203.0*	*250.0*	*71.3*	*64.9*	*45.6*
Volunteer Fire Asst.	*7.9*	*9.0*	*9.0*	*9.0*	*6.4*
Biomass Energy Programs	*0.0*	*55.0*	*5.0*	*5.0*	*5.0*
DOI Rural Assistance	5.9	7.0	7.0	0.0	0.0
Total Wildfire Funds	**216.7**	**321.0**	**87.3**	**78.9**	**56.9**
Forest Service, S&PF	38.5	41.0	46.1	39.0	40.2
State Fire Assistance	*32.6*	*35.0*	*39.1*	*32.4*	*33.2*
Volunteer Fire Asst.	*5.9*	*6.0*	*7.0*	*6.7*	*7.0*
Total Assistance for Nonfederal Lands	**255.3**	**362.1**	**133.4**	**117.9**	**97.1**
FS, Wildfire Mgt.	69.3	59.1	64.1	64.0	48.3
Joint Fire Science	*7.9*	*8.0*	*8.0*	*8.0*	*7.3*
Fire research	*23.5*	*23.9*	*23.9*	*23.9*	*21.7*
Fire facilities	*14.0*	*0.0*	*0.0*	*0.0*	*0.0*
Forest health	*23.9*	*27.2*	*32.2*	*32.1*	*19.3*
DOI	12.0	12.1	12.1	12.1	12.1
Joint Fire Science	*5.9*	*6.0*	*6.0*	*6.0*	*6.0*
Fire facilities	*6.1*	*6.1*	*6.1*	*6.1*	*6.1*
Total Wildfire Funds for Other Purposes	**81.3**	**71.2**	**76.0**	**76.1**	**60.5**

Source: Annual agency budget justifications and conference agreements on P.L. 110-
116, P.L. 110-161, P.L. 110- 329, P.L. 111-5, P.L. 111-8, and P.L. 111-88.
[a] Includes funding in P.L. 111-5, the American Recovery and Reinvestment Act of
2009—$200.0 million in FS State Fire Assistance and $50.0 million in Biomass
Energy Programs—although the funds could be spent in FY2009 or FY2010.
[b] Includes 0.2% across-the-board reduction.

Other Fire Funding

Wildfire appropriations are also provided for several other activities,
including wildfire research, construction and maintenance of fire facilities, and

forest health management, as shown in Table 3 and Table 4. Wildfire funds for fire research have been enacted for both DOI and the FS for the Joint Fire Science program. For FY2012, the request matched the DOI FY2009, FY2010, and FY2011 appropriations and reduced the proposed FS funding by 9%. The FS also has been appropriated wildfire funds for fire plan research and development, beginning in FY2001 and averaging more than $22 million annually; for FY2012, the request was $22 million. These funds supplement monies for wildfire research in the FS research account, but the amount of FS research funding for wildfire research is not specified.

Both DOI and the FS have received funds to improve deteriorating fire facilities. The BLM long used a portion of its fire preparedness funds for "deferred maintenance and capital improvements" (i.e., for fire facilities), but the level fluctuated. DOI's FY2012 request matched the annual appropriations of $6 million for FY2008 through FY2011. FS wildfire funds for fire facilities declined after the initial $43.9 million in FY2001 and ended in FY2004, except for $14.0 million of emergency funds in FY2008. The FS also builds and maintains fire facilities with its capital construction and maintenance account, but the portion used for fire facilities is unknown.

Finally, the FS has received wildfire funds for forest health management. This S&PF program focuses on assessing and controlling insect and disease infestations on federal and cooperative (i.e., nonfederal) lands, but includes efforts to control invasive species. In FY2001 and FY2002, the FS received nearly $12 million annually in wildfire funds for forest health management. Appropriations rose to nearly $25 million in FY2004, and have generally remained near that level. For FY2010 and FY2011, appropriations rose to $32 million of wildfire funding for forest health management, but the FY2012 request dropped to $19 million. (The S&PF funding for forest health management was proposed to decline by 6%.)

FIRE FUNDING ISSUES

Four issues related to wildfire funding have arisen in the last few years. The one receiving the most congressional attention is the high cost of wildfire management and its effect on other aspects of federal land management. Another issue is the level of fire protection funding to reduce fuel loads on federal lands. A third, related issue is the federal role in fire protection of nonfederal lands and structures, and the funding of the relevant federal activities. During the 109th Congress and again recently, a fourth issue was raised, about post-fire rehabilitation.

Wildfire Management Costs

Federal costs for wildfire management are substantially higher than they were in the 1990s, as shown in Figure 2. Federal wildfire appropriations averaged $1.1 billion for FY1994-FY1999, and ranged from $772 million to $1.4 billion. For FY2004-FY2009, federal wildfire appropriations averaged $3.4 billion—more than three times above the FY1994-FY1999 average—and ranged from $2.7 billion to $4.5 billion. (The data are not adjusted for inflation.) Furthermore, the higher costs seem to be continuing, since FY2008 and FY2009 had the highest wildfire funding in history. This has been followed by lower FY2010 and FY2011 appropriations and FY2012 requests, but funding has not declined as much as the decline in area burned.

Management costs have risen in response to increasingly severe wildfire seasons, as shown in Figure 1. The average acreage burned was 3.32 million acres annually for 1990-1999 and 6.93 million acres annually for 2000-2009.[12] The six biggest fire seasons of the past 50 years—2000, 2002, 2004, 2005, 2006, and 2007—have occurred in the past decade. The threat of severe wildfires and the costs of fire protection have grown because many forests have unnaturally high amounts of biomass to fuel the fires (discussed further below). Increased costs have also been attributed to the increasing numbers of homes and people in and near forests—the *wildland-urban interface*.[13] As more people and valuable homes are exposed to wildfire threats, the costs to suppress wildfires to protect those people and houses rises substantially.

Wildfire management has also become relatively more important for the agencies. In addition to the absolute rise in wildfire management costs, a greater share of discretionary appropriations have been spent on wildfire management in recent years. For FY1993-FY2000, wildfire management appropriations were 25% of discretionary appropriations for the FS, ranging from 16% in FY1993 to 30% in FY1997.[14] However, for FY2003 through FY2011, wildfire management funding averaged 47% of discretionary FS appropriations, ranging from 42% in FY2006 to 56% in FY2008. (The FY2012 budget request included 37% of discretionary funding for wildfire management.) Concerns have focused on the continued high costs of wildfire management, especially of fire suppression expenditures, and on the indirect effects of those high costs on other agency management programs.

Continued High Costs

Numerous organizations have examined wildfire suppression costs and made recommendations to the agencies for how to contain those costs.[15] These reports present three general conclusions: (1) a fair share of wildfire suppression should be paid by state and/or local governments; (2) more, better, and better-focused fuel reduction efforts are needed (discussed below); and (3) better accountability for cost control is needed.

Several reports have noted that wildfire suppression cost-share agreements are inconsistent and inequitable, and that cost apportionment and responsibilities among the various levels of government are unclear. This has led to increasing reliance by homeowners and local governments on federal fire protection, despite the relatively clear direction in the 1995 federal fire policy review to increase local responsibility for wildfire protection and suppression for nonfederal lands and structures.[16] The reports note that significant local cost responsibility is necessary to give incentives to homeowners and local governments to take actions to protect themselves, and that without such incentives, federal costs will continue to escalate.

The reports also discuss the need for better cost control and accountability. Most have noted the inconsistent cost tracking and the weak measures of the benefits of fire suppression efforts. GAO noted:[17]

> the agencies need to establish clear goals, strategies, and performance measures to help contain wildland fire costs. Although the agencies have taken certain steps to help contain wildland fire costs, the effectiveness of these steps may be limited because agencies have not established clear cost containment goals for the wildland fire program, including how containing costs should be considered in relation to other wildland fire program goals such as protecting lives, resources, and property; strategies to achieve these goals; or effective performance measures to track their progress.

Another part of cost control and accountability is integrating wildfire management in land and resource planning and in budgeting. One aspect of this integration is maintaining local capacity for initial attack on new wildfires. Most of the reports assert that, without that local capacity, new fires could grow into additional conflagrations if resources are too focused on suppressing current large fires. However, the very high cost of implementing this vision (essentially the 10-acre policy of the 1920s) and lack of evidence of the benefits led the agencies to abandon this approach for wildfire planning in the 1970s.

This leads to questions about the effectiveness of fire suppression. The Strategic Issues Panel noted that the high cost of large fires was the result of the "unwillingness to take greater risks, unwillingness to recognize that suppression techniques are sometimes futile, the 'free' nature of wildland fire suppression funding, and public and political expectations."[18] FS policy results in fire managers generally not being held accountable for "excess" spending on fire control or for fire damages if they clearly put forth valiant efforts to control the conflagration. However, they are blamed for fire damages if the fire control efforts are seen as insufficient—too few people, too little equipment, not enough air tanker drops, or similar problems. The Strategic Issues Panel recommended better fire cost data and "a benefit cost measure as the core measure of suppression cost effectiveness."[19]

Indirect Effects on Agency Programs
Wildfire suppression appropriations—including emergency supplemental funding—exceeded $1 billion for the first time in FY2001, and have remained above $1 billion annually since FY2003, exceeding $2.4 billion in FY2008. Furthermore, wildfire suppression expenditures have exceeded agency appropriations annually for more than a decade. How can an agency spend more than its appropriations? In most situations, it can't. However, provisions in the annual Interior appropriations acts authorized DOI and the FS to borrow unobligated funds from other accounts for emergency firefighting. This, in effect, was an open-ended reprogramming authority.

Historically, the authority to borrow funds from other accounts was not a significant problem. The FS has several mandatory spending accounts, funded primarily from timber receipts; prior to 1990, several of these accounts had substantial running balances. One, the Knutson-Vandenberg (K-V) Fund, was particularly useful, since it had a running balance of about $500 million (about three years of spending).[20] Firefighting funds could be borrowed from the K-V Fund (or other accounts), and repaid later with regular or supplemental appropriations, without a significant effect on agency activities, such as reforestation. The decline in timber sales since 1990 has led to a comparable decline in K-V (and other mandatory spending account) balances, and thus the FS has had to turn to other accounts to borrow funds to pay for firefighting.

Another reason why the borrowing authority was not a problem historically is that, prior to FY2000, there were more discretionary funds to borrow. As noted above, FY1993-FY2000 wildfire management appropriations averaged 25% of discretionary FS appropriations for the FS, leaving significant funds in other accounts to borrow from. (This is less of an issue for DOI, since it can borrow from any DOI accounts.) However, since FY2001, fire management expenditures have averaged 47% of discretionary FS appropriations, and totaled 56% of FS discretionary appropriations in FY2008. Thus, there were relatively fewer funds available to borrow, and borrowing to pay for firefighting was having a relatively greater effect on those other accounts. Various interests increasingly expressed concerns about the effects of firefighting borrowing on the agencies' abilities to implement other programs.

Legislation was introduced to address the situation. Freestanding bills in the 110th and 111th Congresses sought to establish a separate fund for major wildfire suppression efforts. One, the Federal Land Assistance, Management and Enhancement (FLAME) Act, was enacted in Title V of P.L. 111-88. It established separate FLAME Wildfire Suppression Reserve Funds for the FS and DOI, to be funded from annual appropriations. The FLAME funds can be used if the Secretary declares that (1) an individual wildfire covers at least 300 acres or threatens lives, property, or resources, or (2) cumulative wildfire suppression and emergency response costs will exceed, within 30 days, appropriations for wildfire suppression and emergency responses. It also directed the Secretaries to report annually on use of the funds, and to report on estimated suppression costs periodically through the year. The funds terminate if there have been no appropriations to or withdrawals from the accounts for three consecutive fiscal years. In addition, the FLAME Act required the agencies to prepare a "cohesive wildland fire management strategy" as recommended by the GAO, and to revise the cohesive strategy at least every five years.[21]

The FLAME funds effectively insulate federal land and resource management programs from the financial impacts of borrowing to pay for wildfire suppression efforts. However, they do not reduce the effects of lost resource management time when agency personnel are assigned to wildfire suppression efforts. In addition, this approach offers no incentives to fire managers to reduce or constrain the costs of fire-fighting efforts, and thus is unlikely to reduce wildfire suppression costs.

Fuel Reduction Funding[22]

Since 1990, recognition of unnaturally high fuel loads of dead trees, dense understories of trees and other vegetation, and non-native species has spurred interest in fuel management activities. This substantial fuel accumulation has

Table 5. Lands At Risk of Ecological Damage from Wildfire
due to Excessive Fuel Levels (millions of acres)

Landowner	Total Acreage	Low Risk	Moderate Risk	High Risk
Forest Service	196.52	64.95	80.45	51.12
Dept. of the Interior	227.72	128.42	75.83	23.47
Other federal, state, & private lands	825.01	404.60	313.54	107.18
Total	1,249.25	597.97	469.82	181.77

Source: Kirsten M. Schmidt et al., *Development of Coarse-Scale Spatial Data for Wildland Fire and Fuel Management*, Gen. Tech. Rept. RMRS-87 (Fort Collins, CO: USDA Forest Service, April 2002), pp. 13-15.

been attributed to various causes: past land management practices (through grazing and logging that altered the vegetation); successful historic fire suppression (by reducing surface fires that burned small-diameter fuels); decreased logging (by reducing removals of burnable materials); climate change (by exacerbating drought and insect and disease infestations and raising ambient air temperatures); and other factors that affect the ecological health of forests.[23] Table 5 shows the acreage, by ownership class, of lands at low, moderate, and high risk of significant ecological damage from wildfire due to high fuel loads.

Fuel Reduction Efforts

Fuel reduction efforts, as discussed above, are commonly proposed as a means of reducing wildfire suppression costs. Fuel management is a collection of activities—primarily prescribed burning and thinning—intended to reduce the threat of significant damages by wildfires. Fuel treatment acreage increased after the mid-1990s. (Earlier data were not reported comparably.) Table 6 shows that the acreage treated from FY1995 to FY2004 increased by 400%. However, treatment acreage fell in FY2005 and again in FY2006, and has not been proposed to return to the FY2004 level. Data on treatments since FY2007 are not included in Table 6, because the FS and DOI revised their reporting systems to include acreage of *wildland fire use* (natural wildfires that are allowed to burn within the prescriptions of fire plans) as fuel treatments; previous data did not include wildland fire use acreage. Furthermore, with the FY2012 FS proposal to transfer fuel reduction on lands not in the WUI to a new National Forest System line item (Integrated Resource Restoration), tracking total fuel reduction efforts would become more difficult.

Fuel reduction may have increased in FY2008 and FY2009, as funding (including under the economic stimulus legislation) continued to rise. (See Table 1 and Table 2.) However, the annual fuel treatment acreage appears to have stabilized at less than 3 million acres annually. At this average treatment level, it would take nearly 25 years to treat the FS and DOI lands at high risk of ecological damage from wildfire, and another 52 years to treat the lands at moderate risk. Furthermore, the FY2010 and FY2011 appropriations for fuel reduction were below the FY2008 and FY2009 levels, and the FY2012 budget request is lower than any funding level since FY2004.

Funding might not be the only limiting factor for fuel treatment. Increasing fuel reduction activities was one of the primary rationales for enacting the Healthy Forests Restoration Act of 2000 (HFRA; P.L. 108-148). Many observers described the need for expeditious action to reduce fuel loads and fuel ladders,[24] and the difficulties in achieving expeditious action because of the environmental documentation and public participation required by the National Environmental Policy Act of 1969 (NEPA; P.L. 91-190, 42 U.S.C. §§4321-4347). HFRA established an expedited process for environmental review and public involvement in fuel reduction activities. In addition, the FS and DOI established categorical exclusions (CEs) from NEPA for hazardous fuel reduction activities; however, in December 2007, the Ninth Circuit Court of Appeals ruled that the CE violated NEPA, and stopped the use of that CE

Table 6. Total Acreage of Fuel Treatment, FY1995-FY2008 (thousands of acres)

	FY1995	FY1996	FY1997	FY1998	FY1999	FY2000	FY2001
FS	541.3	599.5	1,097.7	1,489.3	1,280.0	772.0	1,361.7
DOI	57.0	298.0	474.0	632.0	827.8	1,020.0	728.1
Total	598.3	897.5	1,571.6	2,121.3	2,107.8	1,792.0	2,089.8
						FY2007	FY2008
	FY2002	FY2003	FY2004	FY2005	FY2006	Planned	Proposed
FS	1,257.9	1,453.3	1,803.8	1,663.9	1,454.7	1,750.0	1,800.0
DOI	1,059.0	1,258.8	1,205.9	1,269.4	1,106.1	1,055.0	1,061.0
Total	2,316.9	2,712.2	3,064.7	2,933.3	2,560.8	2,805.0	2,861.0

Source: Annual agency budget justifications. The agencies no longer report fuel treatment on the same basis, and thus actual treatments since FY2007 cannot be shown.

until NEPA had been followed.[25] It is unclear how much fuel reduction has occurred under either of these authorities. Some oppose expedited actions with limited public oversight, fearing the potential for commercial harvests of large trees (which might provide little or no wildfire protection) and the associated road construction disguised as fuel reduction.

Others have suggested focusing fuel treatment in the wildland-urban interface (WUI), to enhance protection of homes and other structures. The proportion of fuel treatments in the WUI increased after FY2001 (the first year for which such data area available), from 37% (45% for the FS, 22% for DOI) to about 60% from FY2003 to FY2006 (73% for the FS, 42% for DOI), and 70% in FY2008 (83% for the FS, 47% for DOI). Research has documented that reducing fuels close to structures (within about 131 feet) is essential to protecting those structures from wildfire, but that fuel reduction beyond that close-in area (about 2 acres) provides no additional protection for structures.[26]

In addition, GAO testified that the agencies still needed to:[27]

> develop a cohesive strategy that identifies the options and associated funding to reduce fuels and address wildland fire problems.... In 2005 and 2006, because the agencies had not yet developed one, GAO reiterated the need for such a strategy but broadened its focus to better address the interrelated nature of fuel reduction efforts and wildland fire response.

The presumption behind fuel treatment is that lower fuel loads and a lack of fuel ladders will reduce the extent of wildfires, the damages they cause, and the cost of controlling them. Numerous on-the-ground anecdotes support this belief. However, little empirical research has documented this presumption. As noted in one research study, "scant information exists on fuel treatment efficacy for reducing wild-fire severity."[28] This study also found that "fuel treatments moderate extreme fire behavior within treated areas, at least in" frequent fire ecosystems. Others have found different results elsewhere; one study reported "no evidence that prescribed burning in these [southern California] brushlands provides any resource benefit ... in this crown-fire ecosystem."[29] A recent summary of wildfire research reported that, although prescribed burning generally reduced fire severity, mechanical fuel reduction did not consistently reduce fire severity, and that limited research had examined the potential impacts of mechanical fuel reduction with prescribed burning or of commercial logging.[30] Thus, it is unclear whether, or to what extent, increasing fuel treatment funding and efforts will protect communities and ecosystems from damaging wildfires.

Biomass Fuels for Energy

Some have suggested combining the need to reduce potentially hazardous biomass fuels from the forest with the desire to produce renewable energy. Biomass can be used to produce liquid transportation fuels (e.g., ethanol) or to produce heat and electricity (most commonly through cogeneration, also known as combined-heat-and-power). In either case, virtually any biomass can be used to supplant fossil fuels for energy production, and could provide a beneficial use for the fuels that need to be removed from forests.

Some FS fuel reduction funds have been used for wood energy programs. For FY2009-FY2011, $5 million annually was used for biomass grants, authorized in Title II of the Healthy Forests Restoration Act (P.L. 108-148). For FY2011, the administration proposed, but Congress did not fund, $5 million for the Community Wood Energy Program and $15 million for the Forest Biomass to Energy Program, two programs established in the 2008 farm bill (P.L. 110-246). These programs can contribute to fuel reduction for federal forests, since they provide markets for the fuels to be removed, but they are not limited to woody biomass from federal lands, and are also likely to be used to remove woody biomass from nonfederal lands. Furthermore, this relatively limited funding provides very modest markets for the substantial volumes of biomass to be removed from federal lands.

Other federal programs exist to provide incentives for renewable energy production, including from biomass.[31] However, some prohibit the use of biomass from federal lands for the renewable energy targets and incentives.[32] This is due at least partly to concerns about diverting federal woody biomass from traditional markets—lumber, plywood, and pulp and paper—to renewable energy markets. The validity of such concerns was illustrated by the initial payments under USDA's Biomass Crop Assistance Program (BCAP). While the goal was, in part, to stimulate removal of woody biomass waste from the forest, much of the initial funding was spent on transporting wood waste from existing wood production facilities (e.g., sawmills) to energy production facilities; previously such wood waste was sold to pulp mills, particleboard plants, and other such users who were unable to compete against the BCAP subsidies for wood-waste-toenergy.[33] The principal difficulty in using woody biomass from forests is that, while the fuel loads might be very high by historical standards in some ecosystems, they are widely scattered and highly diverse in size and structure, making collection and transport very expensive.

Federal Role in Protecting Nonfederal Lands

The states are responsible for protecting nonfederal lands from wildfires, but FS cooperative fire assistance to states has been authorized since the Clarke-McNary Act of 1924. Cooperative fire assistance was questioned during the Reagan, George H. W. Bush, and Clinton administrations, with budget proposals to substantially reduce funding (generally to less than 30% of enacted appropriations) from FY1984 through FY1995.

The debate over the federal role in assisting states shifted following the severe fire season in summer of 1994. The *Federal Wildland Fire Management Policy & Program Review: Final Report*, released in December 1995, altered federal fire policy from priority for private property to equal priority for private property and federal resources, based on values at risk. (Protecting human life remains the first priority in firefighting.) The increased emphasis on state and local responsibility for protecting nonfederal lands also led to a recognition of the importance of federal assistance to state and local agencies. (Sharing fire suppression costs with state and local governments is discussed above, under "Wildfire Management Costs.")

In contrast to White House efforts to cut fire assistance funding in the 1980s and early 1990s, federal funding for state and volunteer fire assistance more than tripled in 2001, rising from $27 million to $91 million, pulled along by the broad rise in federal wildfire funding under the National Fire Plan. (See Table 3.) State and volunteer fire assistance funding continued to rise for a few years, peaking at $314 million in FY2009, including the funding in the economic stimulus legislation.

The 2002 farm bill (P.L. 107-171, the Farm Security and Rural Investment Act of 2002) authorized a new fire assistance program, the Community Fire Protection Program. The program authorizes the FS, working with and through state forestry agencies, to assist local fire protection planning, education, and activities. The program was authorized at $35 million annually for FY2002-FY2007, and "such sums as are necessary" thereafter; to date, no explicit budget line items have been enacted for this program.

Questions persist about the appropriate role of federal firefighters and funds in protecting structures, communities, and privately owned resources.[34] States bear the responsibility for fire protection on all nonfederal lands. The FS and others also support the FIREWISE program to educate landowners and communities about how to protect their properties and structures from wildfire. The National Interagency Fire Center coordinates the movement of firefighting forces (federal, state, and private contractors) to areas with lots of wildfires. The federal agencies are also directed to give "excess personal property" (such as surplus firefighting equipment) to state or local fire departments. Some question whether these programs are sufficient; others suggest that perhaps federal financial assistance could be terminated. Still others question federal firefighting actions, where state or local responsibility for structure fires has been used as an excuse for inaction.[35] On the other hand, federal firefighters are not trained to fight structure fires, and such efforts without proper training might endanger the firefighters, it has been argued.

The appropriate federal response following wildfire damages to private lands and resources has also been questioned. Catastrophic wildfires sometimes lead to disaster declarations, and thus to recovery efforts coordinated and assisted by the Federal Emergency Management Agency (FEMA) of the Department of Homeland Security. Wildfire damages not in declared disaster areas are sometimes, but not always, covered by private insurance (which is regulated by the states). Homeowners without fire insurance or whose fire insurance does not cover wildfires may be left without compensation for their losses. Similarly, landowners with resource losses (e.g., many trees killed by wildfire) may receive no compensation or assistance to help recover from the losses. It seems unfair to some that wildfire damages are substantially covered only when total damages are sufficient to declare the area a disaster. To address these concerns, some have suggested that the National Flood Insurance Program might provide an appropriate model for federal wildfire insurance for private landowners.[36] Others assert that private insurance exists and is more efficient than a government insurance program, and that the National Flood Insurance Program has not prevented building in flood zones or repetitive flood losses, despite these being part of its goals.

Post-Fire Rehabilitation

Rehabilitation of burned sites following intense wildfires has been a generally accepted practice. As shown in Table 1 and Table 2, the DOI has traditionally received modest appropriations for rehabilitation of DOI lands, except in FY2001; in contrast, the FS has generally funded burned area rehabilitation from regular appropriations for vegetation management, wildlife habitat, watershed management, and other accounts, with modest appropriations (less than $13 million annually) for rehabilitation except in FY2001, FY2002, and FY2008.

Attention to post-fire rehabilitation has increased since 2000. The Bush administration finalized regulations authorizing NEPA categorical exclusions for post-fire rehabilitation activities affecting up to 4,200 acres in June 2003.[37] These (and other) regulations were successfully challenged as violating the Forest Service Decision Making and Appeals Reform Act (§322 of P.L. 102-381; 16 U.S.C. §1612 note), and the FS suspended many proposed actions in response to the court's order.[38]

Legislation was introduced relating to post-fire rehabilitation in the 109th Congress. One bill that passed the House (H.R. 4200, the Forest Emergency Recovery and Research Act of 2006) would have directed the FS and BLM to establish research protocols for catastrophic events affecting forests, to provide an expedited process for recovery of forests from catastrophic events, and to authorize financial assistance to restore landscapes and communities affected by catastrophic events. The expedited process would have required catastrophic event recovery assessments, with pre-approved management practices and alternative NEPA arrangements, and foreshortened administrative and judicial reviews of related activities. The bill has not been introduced in subsequent Congresses.

More recently, other bills have proposed national or regional post-fire and other forest restoration programs with modified procedures for assessing and implementing practices. The Collaborative Forest Landscape Restoration Act was included as Title IV in the Omnibus Public Lands Management Act of 2009 (P.L. 111-11). It provides a collaborative (diverse, multi-party) process for geographically dispersed, long-term (10-year), large-scale (at least 50,000-acre) strategies to restore forests, reduce wildfire threats, and utilize the available biomass, with multi-party monitoring of and reporting on activities. For FY2012, the Obama administration has requested funding for this program as part of a new line item (Integrated Resource Restoration) within the National Forest System appropriation account. Other bills typically address specific areas or specific restoration needs.

Post-fire rehabilitation needs and funding have arisen again in the 112th Congress, in the wake of the worst wildfire in Arizona history. Attention is being given to the burned area emergency response (BAER) program—authorized activities, funding mechanisms, public involvement, and more. To date, no legislation has been introduced, nor have any oversight hearings been held or scheduled. Nonetheless, given the importance of the process and the concerns about conditions, the BAER program may receive congressional consideration in the 112th Congress.

No data or assessments have examined the adequacy of current rehabilitation activities. It is unclear how often rehabilitation activities are necessary or feasible. It is also unclear whether NEPA environmental reviews or public involvement have delayed rehabilitation activities significantly. Opponents of legislated changes to existing environmental review and public involvement processes have expressed concerns that changes could reduce review and oversight of salvage logging decisions, since salvage logging is not generally precluded as a rehabilitation activity. They note that salvage logging can cause significant environmental damage. Proponents of changes contend that timber salvage can help in site rehabilitation, both by reducing costs and by removing dead biomass that may interfere with vegetative regrowth on the site, and that expedited processes are necessary to utilize the timber before it deteriorates.

APPENDIX. ACRES BURNED AND FUNDING DATA

Table A-1. Acres Burned in Wildfires Since 1960
(millions of acres)

Year	Acres	Year	Acres	Year	Acres
1960	4.48	1977	3.15	1994	4.07
1961	3.04	1978	3.91	1995	1.84
1962	4.08	1979	2.99	1996	6.07
1963	7.12	1980	5.26	1997	2.86
1964	4.20	1981	4.81	1998	1.33
1965	2.65	1982	2.38	1999	5.63
1966	4.57	1983	1.32	2000	7.39
1967	4.66	1984	1.15·	2001	3.57
1968	4.23	1985	2.90	2002	7.18
1969	6.69	1986	2.72	2003	3.96
1970	3.28	1987	2.45	2004	8.10
1971	4.28	1988	5.01	2005	8.69
1972	2.64	1989	1.83	2006	9.87
1973	1.92	1990	4.62	2007	9.33
1974	2.88	1991	2.95	2008	5.29
1975	1.79	1992	2.07	2009	5.92
1976	5.11	1993	1.80	2010	3.42

Source: National Interagency Fire Center, at http://www.nifc.gov/fire_info /fires_acres.htm.

Note: Data for 1983-1991 have been revised downward.

Table A-1 presents the data on acres burned annually in the United States since 1960. These data are presented graphically in Figure 1.

Table A-2 presents data on the total appropriations to the FS and DOI wildland fire management accounts. These data are presented graphically in Figure 2.

Table A-2. Total Appropriations to Wildfire Accounts, FY1994-FY2011 ($ in millions)

	FY1994	FY1995	FY1996	FY1997	FY1998	FY1999	FY2000
FS	752.7	835.6	485.5	1,080.0	836.6	722.4	1,008.0
DOI	350.5	235.7	286.9	352.0	280.1	336.9	591.0
Total	1,103.2	1,071.3	772.4	1,432.1	1,116.7	1,059.3	1,598.9
	FY2001	FY2002	FY2003	FY2004	FY2005	FY2006	FY2007
FS	1,882.8	1,560.3	2,290.0	2,347.0	2,128.5	1,846.1	2,193.6
DOI	977.1	678.4	875.2	883.6	831.3	855.3	853.4
Total	2,859.9	2,238.8	3,165.1	3,230.6	2,929.8	2,701.4	3,047.0
				FY2011	FY2012		
	FY2008a	FY2009b	FY2010c	enactedd	request		
FS	3,269.5	2,831.6	2,516.7	2,058.5	1,830.9e		
DOI	1,192.1	924.5	855.9	778.9	821.5		
Total	4,461.5	3,756.1	3,372.6	2,837.4	2,652.5		

Note: Totals in this table are the sum of totals in Table 1, Table 2, Table 3, and Table 4, excluding the wildfire assistance programs funded through FS State and Private Forestry. The numbers may not add to the total due to rounding error.

[a] Includes emergency supplemental appropriations in P.L. 110-116 (Div. B), P.L. 110-161 (Div. F, Title V), and P.L. 110-329 (Div. B), as well as regular FY2008 appropriations in P.L. 110-161.

[b] Includes supplemental appropriations in P.L. 111-32 and funds in P.L. 111-5, the American Recovery and Reinvestment Act; the latter funds, $500.0 million for the FS and $15.0 million for DOI, were available to be spent in FY2009 or FY2010, but are shown in FY2009 funding.

[c] Reduced by $75.0 million of prior-year FS funds and $125.0 million of prior-year DOI funds.

[d] Reflects rescissions of $400.0 million for the FS and $200.0 million for DOI, and a 0.2% across-the-board reduction.

[e] Reflects a reduction of $192.0 million in hazardous fuels treatment and a rescission of $192.0 million, as reported by the House Appropriations Subcommittee on Interior, Environment, and Related Agencies; the FS FY2012 budget justification does not show the $192.0 million reduction in hazardous fuels treatment.

End Notes

[1] Stephen J. Pyne, "Keynote Address," in *The Fires Next Time: Transcript* (Boise, ID: Andrus Center for Public Policy, 2001), pp. 2-7.

[2] See Julie K. Gorte and Ross W. Gorte, *Application of Economic Techniques to Fire Management—A Status Review and Evaluation*, Gen. Tech. Rept. INT-53 (Ogden, UT: USDA Forest Service, June 1979).

[3] Stephen J. Pyne, *Fire In America: A Cultural History of Wildland and Rural Fire* (Princeton NJ: Princeton University Press, 1982), pp. 293-294.

[4] R. Neil Sampson, chair, *Report of the National Commission on Wildfire Disasters* (Washington, DC: 1994).

[5] Bob Armstrong, Assistant Secretary for Lands and Minerals Management, U.S. Dept. of the Interior, "Statement," *Fire Policy and Related Forest Health Issues*, joint oversight hearing, House Committees on Resources and on Agriculture, October 4, 1994 (Washington, DC: U.S. GPO, 1995), p. 9. Serials No. 103-119 (Committee on Resources) and 103-82 (Committee on Agriculture).

[6] GAO, *Western National Forests: A Cohesive Strategy Is Needed to Address Catastrophic Wildfire Threats*, GAO/RCED-99-65 (Washington, DC: April 1999), hereinafter cited as GAO, *Cohesive Strategy Needed*; and GAO, *Federal Wildfire Activities: Current Strategy and Issues Needing Attention*, GAO/RCED-99-233 (Washington, DC: August 1999).

[7] U.S. Government Accountability Office, Wildland Fire Management: Federal Agencies Have Taken Important Steps Forward, but Additional, Strategic Action is Needed to Capitalize on Those Steps, GAO-09-877, September 9, 2009, http://www.gao.gov/new.items/d09877.pdf.

[8] See CRS Report R40811, *Wildfire Fuels and Fuel Reduction*, by Ross W. Gorte.

[9] This is the amount reported by the House Appropriations Subcommittee on Interior, Environment, and Related Agencies; the FS FY2012 budget justification shows $254 million for this activity.

[10] For more details on these programs, see CRS Report RL31065, *Forestry Assistance Programs*, by Ross W. Gorte.

[11] See CRS Report R40529, *Biomass: Comparison of Definitions in Legislation Through the 111th Congress*, by Kelsi Bracmort and Ross W. Gorte.

[12] Acreage burned is a common measure to assess fire season severity, but larger fires are not necessarily "worse" if they burn less intensely, because their damages may be lower. However, fire intensity and damages are not measured consistently, and thus cannot be used to gauge the severity of a fire season. It is unknown whether acreage burned might provide a reasonable approximation of fire season severity.

[13] See CRS Report RS21880, *Wildfire Protection in the Wildland-Urban Interface*, by Ross W. Gorte.

[14] CRS calculations from data in the annual FS budget justifications.

[15] The organizations' reports include GAO, *Cohesive Strategy Needed*; GAO, *Wildland Fire Management: Lack of a Cohesive Strategy Hinders Agencies' Cost-Containment Efforts*, GAO-07-427T (Washington, DC: January 30, 2007), 13 p.; and more than a dozen other GAO reports; National Academy on Public Administration, *Wildfire Suppression: Strategies for Containing Costs* (Washington, DC: September 2002), 2 volumes; Strategic Issues Panel on Fire Suppression Cost, *Large Fire Suppression Costs: Strategies for Cost Management, A Report to the Wildland Fire Leadership Council* (August 26, 2004), available at http://www.forestsandrangelands.gov/reports/documents/2004/ cost management.pdf, hereinafter cited as *Large Fire Suppression Costs: Strategies for Cost*

Management; and U.S. Dept. of Agriculture, Office of Inspector General, Western Region, *Audit Report: Forest Service Large Fire Suppression Costs*, Rept. No. 08601-44-SF (November 2006), 47 p.

[16] U.S. Dept. of the Interior and Dept. of Agriculture, *Federal Wildland Fire Management Policy & Program Review: Final Report* (Washington, DC: December 18, 1995).

[17] Senate ENR, *Hearing on Wildfire Suppression Costs*, p. 15.

[18] *Large Fire Suppression Costs: Strategies for Cost Management*, p. 6.

[19] *Large Fire Suppression Costs: Strategies for Cost Management*, p. 33.

[20] The Act of June 9, 1930 (16 U.S.C. §§576-576b), authorizes the FS to require deposits from timber purchasers to cover the cost of reforestation, timber stand improvement, and other resource mitigation and enhancement of timber sale areas. See CRS Report RL30335, *Federal Land Management Agencies' Mandatory Spending Authorities*, coordinated by Ross W. Gorte.

[21] As enacted in P.L. 111-88, the FLAME Act did not include two provisions of H.R. 1404 and S. 561: (1) to report on each wildfire costing more than $10 million, and (2) to authorize grants and cost-sharing agreements for "fire-ready communities" that have taken identified steps to reduce their risk from wildfires.

[22] See CRS Report R40811, *Wildfire Fuels and Fuel Reduction*, by Ross W. Gorte.

[23] See CRS Report RL30755, *Forest Fire/Wildfire Protection*, by Ross W. Gorte.

[24] A *fuel ladder* is a stand structure with continuous fuels, in the form of tall grasses and forbs, shrubs, and low branches, between the ground and the tree crowns that allow surface fires to spread upward.

[25] *Sierra Club v. Bosworth*, 510 F.3d 1016 (9th Cir. 2007).

[26] See CRS Report RS21880, *Wildfire Protection in the Wildland-Urban Interface*, by Ross W. Gorte.

[27] U.S. Congress, Senate Energy and Natural Resources, *Cost of Wildfire Suppression*, 110th Cong., 1st sess., January 30, 2007, S.Hrg. 110-11 (Washington: GPO, 2007), pp. 16-17.

[28] Philip N. Omi and Erik J. Martinson, *Effects of Fuels Treatment on Wildfire Severity: Final Report*, submitted to the Joint Fire Science Program Governing Board (Fort Collins, CO: Colorado State University, Western Forest Fire Research Center, March 25, 2002).

[29] Jon E. Keeley, "Fire Management of California Shrubland Landscapes," *Environmental Management*, vol. 29, no. 3 (2002), pp. 395-408.

[30] Henry Carey and Martha Schumann, *Modifying WildFire Behavior—The Effectiveness of Fuel Treatments: The Status of Out Knowledge*, Southwest Region Working Paper 2 (Santa Fe, NM: National Community Forestry Center, April 2003).

[31] See CRS Report RL34130, *Renewable Energy Programs in the 2008 Farm Bill*, by Megan Stubbs; and CRS Report R41106, *Meeting the Renewable Fuel Standard (RFS) Mandate for Cellulosic Biofuels: Questions and Answers*, by Kelsi Bracmort.

[32] See CRS Report R40529, *Biomass: Comparison of Definitions in Legislation Through the 111th Congress*, by Kelsi Bracmort and Ross W. Gorte.

[33] See USDA Commodity Credit Corporation, "Biomass Crop Assistance Program: Proposed Rule," *Federal Register*, v. 75, no. 25 (February 8, 2010), http://www.fsa.usda.gov/Internet /FSA_Federal_Notices/bcap_prm_2_8_2010.pdf.

[34] See CRS Report RL34517, *Wildfire Damages to Homes and Resources: Understanding Causes and Reducing Losses*, by Ross W. Gorte, and CRS Report RS21880, *Wildfire Protection in the Wildland-Urban Interface*, by Ross W. Gorte.

[35] At least two houses on the Standing Rock Indian Reservation burned down in the summer of 2006, because firefighters of the Bureau of Indian Affairs apparently were not allowed to

fight fires in private dwellings, only grassland fires and government structure fires; the policy was modified in July 2006 ("Dorgan: BIA Changing Policy on Standing Rock Fires," *Associated Press*, July 15, 2006).

[36] See CRS Report RS22394, *National Flood Insurance Program: Treasury Borrowing in the Aftermath of Hurricane Katrina*, by Rawle O. King.

[37] 68 *Fed. Reg.* 33814 (June 5, 2003).

[38] *Earth Island v. Pengilly*, 376 F.Supp. 2d 994 (E.D.Cal. 2005).

In: Federal Firefighter Funding and Fire Assistance   ISBN 978-1-62081-176-4
Editors: M. L. Hill and C. F. Green   ©2012 Nova Science Publishers, Inc.

Chapter 4

FEDERAL ASSISTANCE FOR WILDFIRE RESPONSE AND RECOVERY[*]

Ross W. Gorte

Raging wildfires, burned homes, and the evacuation of thousands make headlines nearly every fire season. Severe wildfires in 2011 occurred in Arizona and New Mexico in the late spring, and in Texas and Arizona in the late summer. Options for federal support and assistance—during the fires, in the aftermath, and aimed at preventing a recurrence—have been raised by many concerned about the ongoing disasters. This report briefly describes these federal options.

DURING THE FIRE

Federal wildfire policy is to actively suppress all wildfires, unless a fire management plan identifies locations and conditions when monitoring or less aggressive suppression efforts are appropriate (called *appropriate management response* or AMR). Federal responsibility for wildfire suppression is to protect lives, property, and resources on federal lands; federal firefighting is funded through the U.S. Forest Service (Department of

---

[*] This is an edited, reformatted and augmented version of Congressional Research Service, Publication No. R41858, dated September 6, 2011.

Agriculture) and through the Department of the Interior.[1] States are responsible for suppressing wildfires on nonfederal (state and private) lands.[2] The federal government provides support to the states in two ways. One is through direct financial assistance for state fire protection efforts, funded through the Forest Service's state fire assistance program. The other, and more critical when wildfires are burning, consists of fire suppression forces and assistance—personnel, funding, and equipment (including aircraft)—provided at a state's request, and coordinated through the National Interagency Fire Center (NIFC) in Boise, ID. In emergencies, NIFC coordinates federal, state, and private forces (including the military, when called upon) to assist the state or region in need while maintaining local wildfire protection; how paying for these forces gets allocated is usually addressed after the emergency is over. The Federal Emergency Management Agency (FEMA) of the Department of Homeland Security can also assist through Fire Management Assistance Grants (FMAGs) that can provide grants, equipment, personnel, and supplies to supplement community resources when fires threaten destruction that might warrant a major disaster declaration; this requires a request from the governor while the fire is burning.[3] If the president declares a disaster, fire management assistance and other recovery programs are also available from FEMA under the Robert T. Stafford Disaster Relief and Emergency Assistance Act.[4]

The federal government also supports state and local efforts to evacuate areas threatened by wildfires. Presidential declaration of an emergency triggers federal aid to protect property and public health and safety while preserving state autonomy and responsibility.[5] Although the new national response framework, required in the wake of Hurricane Katrina, is still not complete, FEMA and the National Guard have been assisting state and local agencies in evacuating areas and establishing and maintaining evacuation shelters.

IN THE AFTERMATH

As with fire control efforts, federal actions in the aftermath of a wildfire disaster can take two principal forms. In the first, a presidential declaration of a major disaster initiates a process for federal assistance to help state and local governments and families and individuals recover from the disaster. The nature and extent of the assistance depends on a number of factors, such as the nature and severity of the wildfire damages and the insurance coverage of the affected parties.[6]

Site rehabilitation and restoration following fire is the second principal form of support by federal agencies. On federal lands, site rehabilitation routinely occurs as an emergency wildfire program and through regular land management activities. Activities include sowing areas with quick-growing grasses as well as planting trees and other activities to reduce erosion.

On state and private lands, the responsibility lies with the landowner, but federal assistance can be provided through the Forest Service's state fire assistance and other state forestry assistance programs.[7] In addition, USDA has two programs—the Emergency Watershed Protection Program administered by the Natural Resources Conservation Service[8] and the Emergency Conservation Program administered by the Farm Service Agency[9]—that can provide for restoration activities (tree planting, streambank stabilization, and more) following wildfires.

Some severely burned areas (e.g., in southern California) are at risk of landslides during the subsequent rainstorms, even after site restoration efforts. Little can be done to prevent such events, but monitoring can provide warning to homeowners to evacuate the area prior to a landslide, and other federal post-disaster assistance can then become available.

PREVENTING A RECURRENCE

Numerous federal programs provide grants to states and local governments to prepare for wildfire emergencies. The Forest Service provides financial and technical assistance and equipment to states and volunteer fire departments, and to communities for wildfire protection planning. FEMA provides grants and training for firefighting and for community responses to terrorist attacks and natural disasters.[10] Projects to reduce the risk of future fires may also be eligible under FEMA's Pre-Disaster Mitigation Program.[11]

A perhaps bigger question is how to prevent a recurrence of catastrophic fires. The answer is: You can't—drought, lightning, and high winds make extreme wildfires inevitable. Reducing fuel levels can, in some ecosystems, reduce the damages from wildfires and decrease the likelihood of a catastrophic wildfire occurring.[12] However, severe wildfires cannot be prevented in ecosystems that have evolved with wildfire, such as the chaparral of southern California and lodgepole pine in the northern and central Rockies. Nonetheless, it is also possible to protect structures in such settings. Federal research and grants, particularly for the FIREWISE program, have shown how homeowners can protect their structures, even while wildfires burn around them.[13] The keys are the structure itself (especially non-flammable roofing) and the landscaping within 40 meters of the structure. Zoning could inform and enforce appropriate standards for wildfire protection for structures.

End Notes

[1] See CRS Report RL33990, Federal Funding for Wildfire Control and Management, by Ross W. Gorte.

[2] See CRS Report RL30755, Forest Fire/Wildfire Protection, by Ross W. Gorte.

[3] See CRS Report RL33053, Federal Stafford Act Disaster Assistance: Presidential Declarations, Eligible Activities, and Funding, by Francis X. McCarthy.

[4] 42 U.S.C. § 5187.

[5] See CRS Report RL34146, FEMA's Disaster Declaration Process: A Primer, by Francis X. McCarthy.

[6] See CRS Report RL31734, Federal Disaster Recovery Programs: Brief Summaries, by Carolyn V. Torsell.

[7] See CRS Report RL31065, Forestry Assistance Programs, by Ross W. Gorte.

[8] 33 U.S.C. § 701b-1 and 16 U.S.C. § 2203. See http://www.nrcs.usda.gov/programs/ewp/.

[9] 16 U.S.C. §§ 2201-2204. See http://www.fsa.usda.gov/FSA/webapp?area= home& subject=copr&topic=ecp.

[10] See CRS Report RS21302, Assistance to Firefighters Program, by Lennard G. Kruger, and CRS Report R40471, FEMA's Hazard Mitigation Grant Program: Overview and Issues, by Natalie Keegan.

[11] 42 U.S.C. § 5133.

[12] See CRS Report R40811, Wildfire Fuels and Fuel Reduction, by Ross W. Gorte.

[13] See CRS Report RS21880, Wildfire Protection in the Wildland-Urban Interface, by Ross W. Gorte.

In: Federal Firefighter Funding and Fire Assistance   ISBN 978-1-62081-176-4
Editors: M. L. Hill and C. F. Green   ©2012 Nova Science Publishers, Inc.

Chapter 5

UNITED STATES FIRE ADMINISTRATION: AN OVERVIEW[*]

Lennard G. Kruger

SUMMARY

The U.S. Fire Administration (USFA)—which includes the National
Fire Academy (NFA)—is currently housed within the Federal Emergency
Management Agency (FEMA) of the Department of Homeland Security
(DHS). The objective of the USFA is to significantly reduce the nation's
loss of life from fire, while also achieving a reduction in property loss and
non-fatal injury due to fire. The United States Fire Administration
Reauthorization Act of 2008 was signed into law on October 8, 2008
(P.L. 110-376).

The Department of Defense and Continuing Appropriations Act,
2011 (P.L. 112-10) funded USFA at $45.588 million, the same as the
FY2010 level. The FY2012 budget proposal requested $42.538 million
for USFA, about 7% under the FY2011 level. The budget proposal
reflected an overall $1.72 million program reduction. P.L. 112-74, the
Consolidated Appropriations Act, FY2012, provided $44.038 million for
USFA in FY2012.

As is the case with many federal programs, concerns in the 112th
Congress over the federal budget deficit could impact budget levels for the
USFA. Debate over the USFA budget has focused on whether the USFA

---

[*] This is an edited, reformatted and augmented version of Congressional Research Service,
Publication No. RS20071, dated January 3, 2012.

is receiving an appropriate level of funding to accomplish its mission, given that appropriations for USFA have consistently been well below the agency's authorized level. An ongoing issue is the viability and status of the USFA and National Fire Academy within the Department of Homeland Security.

BACKGROUND

The U.S. Fire Administration (USFA) is currently an entity within the Federal Emergency Management Agency (FEMA) of the Department of Homeland Security (DHS). Its mission is to provide leadership, coordination, and support for the nation's fire prevention and control, fire training and education, and emergency medical services activities, and to prepare first responders and health care leaders to react to all hazard and terrorism emergencies of all kinds. One of USFA's key objectives is to significantly reduce the nation's loss of life from fire, while also achieving a reduction in property loss and non-fatal injury due to fire. Although fire loss has improved significantly over the past 25 years, the fire problem in the United States remains serious. The United States still has one of the highest fire death rates in the industrialized world. According to the National Fire Protection Association (NFPA), in 2010 there were 3,120 civilian fire deaths, 17,720 civilian fire injuries, and an estimated $11.6 billion in property damage.[1] According to the NFPA, there were 72 on-duty firefighter deaths in 2010.[2]

The genesis of USFA and FEMA's fire prevention and control activities can be found in the landmark 1973 report of the National Commission on Fire Prevention and Control,[3] entitled *America Burning*. The commission recommended the creation of a federal fire agency which would provide support to state and local governments and private fire organizations in their efforts to reduce fire deaths, injuries, and property loss. The commission recommended that this new agency be placed within the Department of Housing and Urban Development. Congress instead opted to place the agency in the Department of Commerce, and with the passage of the Federal Fire Prevention and Control Act of 1974 (P.L. 93-498),[4] the National Fire Prevention and Control Administration (NFPCA) was established. In 1978, Congress changed the name of NFPCA to USFA (P.L. 95-422), and in 1979, President Carter's Reorganization Plan No. 3 placed the USFA within the newly created FEMA. Also in 1979, the National Fire Academy (NFA) in

Emmitsburg, MD, was opened, offering courses and training to fire service personnel and other persons engaged in fire prevention and control.

During the early 1980s, the Reagan administration proposed the elimination of the USFA (while preserving the Fire Academy). Although Congress did not allow the termination of the USFA, the agency suffered severe staff reductions and the Fire Academy was separated from the USFA and housed organizationally with other FEMA emergency training programs. In 1991, the NFA was subsequently reorganized back into the USFA, where it remains today.

Currently, the USFA is located on the grounds of the National Emergency Training Center in Emmitsburg, MD. USFA programs include the following:

Data Collection—USFA's National Fire Data Center (NFDC) administers a national system for collecting, analyzing and disseminating data and information on fire and other emergency incidents to State and local governments and the fire community. The NFDC provides a national analysis of the fire problem, identifying problem areas for which prevention and mitigation strategies are needed.

Public Education and Awareness—Through partnerships and special initiatives, USFA involves the fire service, the media, other federal agencies and safety interest groups in the development and delivery of fire safety awareness and education programs. These programs are targeted at those groups most vulnerable to the hazards of fire, including the young, elderly, and disabled.

Training—USFA's National Fire Academy (NFA) offers educational opportunities for the advanced professional development of the mid-level and senior fire/EMS officer and allied professionals involved in fire prevention and life safety activities. The academy develops and delivers educational and training programs with a national focus that supplement and support State and local fire service training. The NFA also offers training to support the National Incident Management System Integration Center (NIC) and nationwide implementation of the National Incident Management System (NIMS).

Research and Technology—Through research, testing and evaluation, USFA works with public and private entities to promote and improve fire and life safety. Research and special studies are conducted on fire detection, suppression and notification systems as well as issues related to firefighter and emergency responder health and safety. Research results are published and made available to the public free of charge through the USFA Publications Center.

Table 1. Appropriations, U.S. Fire Administration (millions of dollars)

	FY2010 (P.L. 111-83)	FY2011 Admin. Request	FY2011 (P.L. 112-10)	FY2012 Admin. Request	FY2012 (P.L. 112-74)
U.S. Fire Administration	45.588	45.930	45.588	42.538	44.038

BUDGET

In previous years, the USFA, through FEMA, received its yearly appropriation through the House and Senate Appropriations Subcommittees on VA, HUD, and Independent Agencies. Beginning in FY2004, the USFA received its appropriation through the House and Senate Appropriations Subcommittees on Homeland Security. Table 1 shows recent and proposed appropriated funding for USFA.

APPROPRIATIONS

Beginning in FY2004, the USFA was funded through the Preparedness, Mitigation, Response, and Recovery (PMRR) account within the Emergency Preparedness and Response Directorate of the Department of Homeland Security. On July 13, 2005, then-DHS Secretary Michael Chertoff announced a restructuring of DHS, effective October 1, 2005. USFA was removed from the PMRR account and received a separate appropriation (its own line item) under the new DHS Directorate for Preparedness. The FY2007 Department of Homeland Security appropriations bill (P.L. 109-295) transferred the USFA back to the Federal Emergency Management Agency within DHS.

FY2010

The Obama administration's FY2010 budget proposal requested $45.588 million for USFA, an increase of 1.3% from the FY2009 level. The increase would be used for pay inflation and an increased contribution to the DHS Working Capital Fund.

Both the House and Senate Appropriations Committees approved $45.588 million for USFA, the same level as the administration's proposal. The House Appropriations Committee (H.R. 2892; H.Rept. 111-157) designated $9.304 million for the National Fire Academy and $1.419 million to continue implementation of the National Fire Information Reporting System (NFIRS). The Senate Appropriations Committee (S. 1298; S.Rept. 111-31) directed USFA to work with the Department of Agriculture and the Department of the Interior to ensure that compatible data on wildfires are available, and directed USFA to brief the committee on the status of the NFIRS upgrade.

The House passed H.R. 2892, the Department of Homeland Security FY2010 appropriations bill, on June 24, 2009. The Senate passed H.R. 2892 on July 9, 2009. The conference report for the Department of Homeland Security Appropriations Act, 2010 (H.Rept. 111-298) provided $45.588 million for USFA, identical to the levels in both the House- and Senate-passed H.R. 2892. The conferees directed USFA to work with the Department of Agriculture and the Department of the Interior to ensure that compatible data on wildfires are available, and directed USFA to provide a briefing within 30 days on the status of the NFIRS upgrade, including future milestones for measuring progress. The conference report was passed by the House on October 15, by the Senate on October 20, and signed into law, P.L. 111-83, on October 28, 2009.

FY2011

The administration's FY2011 budget proposal requested $45.930 million for USFA, an increase of 0.7% from the FY2010 level. The increase of $342,000 would be used for pay inflation. On July 14, 2010, the House Subcommittee on Homeland Security Appropriations approved $45.930 million, the same level proposed by the administration. On July 19, 2010, the Senate Appropriations Committee also approved $45.930 for the USFA (S. 3607; S.Rept. 111-222).

The Department of Defense and Continuing Appropriations Act, 2011 (P.L. 112-10) funded USFA at the FY2010 level of $45.588 million.

FY2012

The FY2012 budget proposal requested $42.538 million for USFA, about 7% under the FY2011 level. The budget proposal reflects an overall $1.72 million program reduction. Specific decreases include reducing National Fire Academy class deliveries with the result that, according to the budget justification, 13,500 fewer students will be trained. Another decrease would eliminate TV studio/broadcast capabilities that deliver critical information and training to all first responders on the campus site and across the nation. According to the budget justification, such a reduction would affect USFA's capability to transmit critical information and just-in-time training during national and regional disasters, and would require USFA to rely upon private sources to be accessed (if available) in order to reach first-wave responders. Other program reductions include eliminating USFA citizen and fire and life prevention research efforts, reducing response efforts, and eliminating wireless capabilities provided to 25,000 resident students and special group participants in the National Emergency Training Center (NETC) dormitories.

The Department of Homeland Security Appropriations Bill, 2012 (H.R. 2017) was reported by the House Appropriations Committee on May 26, 2011. The House bill would provide $42.538 million for USFA, the same as the administration request. The House Appropriations bill report (H.Rept. 112-91) requested that future budget justifications identify funding levels for the National Fire Academy, the National Fire Incident Reporting System, and any other initiatives. The Department of Homeland Security Appropriations, 2012, bill (H.R. 2017) was passed by the House on June 2, 2011.

On September 7, 2011, the Senate Appropriations Committee approved $45.038 million for USFA in FY2012 (S.Rept. 112-74), which is a 6% increase over the House-passed level and the administration request.

P.L. 112-74, the Consolidated Appropriations Act, FY2012, provided $44.038 million for USFA in FY2012.

Authorizations

The U.S. Fire Administration Reauthorization Act of 2003 (P.L. 108-169) was signed into law on December 6, 2003. The act reauthorized the USFA through FY2008 at the following levels: $63 million for FY2005, $64.85 million for FY2006, $66.796 million for FY2007, and $68.8 million for FY2008. P.L. 108-169 also reestablished the presidentially appointed position of the U.S. Fire Administrator, which had been statutorily abolished by the Homeland Security Act of 2002. Additionally, the legislation directed the USFA to develop new firefighting technologies and standards in coordination with private sector standards groups and federal, state, and local agencies. P.L. 108-169 required that equipment purchased with fire grant money meet or exceed voluntary consensus standards when feasible.

The United States Fire Administration Reauthorization Act of 2008 was signed into law on October 8, 2008 (P.L. 110-376). P.L. 110-376 authorizes the USFA at $70 million for FY2009, $72.1 million for FY2010, $74.263 million for FY2011, and $76.491 million for FY2012. Provisions include authorizing National Fire Academy training program modifications and reports; directing the National Fire Academy to provide training on incidents occurring in the wildfire-urban interface, multi-jurisdictional fires, hazardous materials incidents, and advanced emergency medical services; authorizing USFA to enter into contracts with one or more nationally recognized third-party organizations to deliver training; a report on the feasibility of providing incident command training for fires at ports and in marine environments; national fire incident reporting system upgrades; sponsoring and disseminating research on fire prevention and control at the wildland-urban interface; encouraging adoption of national voluntary consensus standards for firefighter health and safety; establishing a state and local fire service position at the National Operations Center within DHS; providing coordination regarding fire prevention and control and emergency medical services; and expressing congressional support for USFA recommendations for adoption and education regarding sprinklers in commercial and residential buildings.

ASSISTANCE TO FIREFIGHTERS PROGRAM (FIRE ACT GRANTS)[5]

The Assistance to Firefighters Grant (AFG) Program, also known as the FIRE Act grant program, was established by Title XVII of the FY2001 Floyd D. Spence National Defense Authorization Act (P.L. 106-398). The program provides federal grants directly to local fire departments and unaffiliated Emergency Medical Services (EMS) organizations to help address a variety of equipment, training, and other firefighter-related and EMS needs. A related program is the Staffing for Adequate Fire and Emergency Response

Firefighters (SAFER) program, which provides grants for hiring, recruiting, and retaining firefighters.[6]

Since its inception, the fire grant program has been administered by FEMA/USFA (FY2001- FY2003), the Office for Domestic Preparedness (FY2004), the Office of State and Local Government Coordination Preparedness (FY2005), and the Office of Grants and Training in the DHS Directorate for Preparedness (FY2006). Congressional appropriations reports have consistently instructed DHS to maintain USFA involvement in the grant administration process for fire and SAFER grants. The FY2007 DHS Appropriations Act (P.L. 109-295) transferred USFA to FEMA and the fire and SAFER grants to the Grants Program Directorate in FEMA.

ISSUES IN THE 112TH CONGRESS

As is the case with many federal programs, concerns in the 112th Congress over the federal budget deficit could impact budget levels for the USFA. Debate over the USFA budget has focused on whether the USFA is receiving an appropriate level of funding to accomplish its mission, given that appropriations for USFA have consistently been well below the agency's authorized level. An ongoing issue is the viability and status of the USFA and National Fire Academy within the Department of Homeland Security. While supportive of the reorganization of FEMA into DHS, many in the fire service community have cautioned that USFA and NFA programs—which address the day-to-day challenges faced by fire departments—should not be overshadowed in an organization which focuses on homeland security and counterterrorism. Since the establishment of DHS in March 2003, fire service groups have opposed a number of actions DHS has taken with respect to the USFA and NFA. These included the abolishment of the presidentially appointed position of U.S. Fire Administrator (subsequently reestablished by enactment of the USFA Reauthorization Act of 2003); proposed cancellations of some NFA courses in 2003 due to an across-the-board FEMA budget cut (those NFA courses were subsequently restored after fire service protests); and the transfer of the fire grants program from the USFA to the Office for Domestic Preparedness.

End Notes

[1] Karter, Michael J., National Fire Protection Association, *Fire Loss in the United States During 2010*, September 2011, available at http://www.nfpa.org/assets/files/PDF/OS.fireloss.pdf.

[2] National Fire Protection Association, *Firefighter Fatalities in the United States – 2010*, June 2011, available at http://www.nfpa.org/assets/files/PDF/osfff.pdf.

[3] The commission was created by P.L. 90-259, the Fire Research and Safety Act of 1968.

[4] 15 U.S.C. 2201 *et seq.*

[5] For more information on the fire grant program, see CRS Report RL32341, *Assistance to Firefighters Program: Distribution of Fire Grant Funding*, by Lennard G. Kruger.

[6] For more details on the SAFER grant program, see CRS Report RL33375, *Staffing for Adequate Fire and Emergency Response: The SAFER Grant Program*, by Lennard G. Kruger.

INDEX